BBC Active, an imprint of Educational Publishers LLP, part of the Pearson Education Group
Edinburgh Gate, Harlow, Essex CM20 2JE, England

© Educational Publishers LLP 2007

BBC logo © BBC 1996. BBC and BBC ACTIVE are trademarks of the British Broadcasting
Corporation

First edition published 1998. This edition published 2007.
Reprinted 2007.

ISBN-13: 978-1-4066-1260-8

Cover design: Emma Wallace
Cover photograph: foodfolio/Alamy
Insides concept design: Nicolle Thomas
Commissioning editor: Debbie Marshall
Project editor: Melanie Kramers
Project assistant: Hannah Beatson
Senior production controller: Man Fai Lau
Layout: Johanna Boyle
Marketing: Fiona Griffiths, Paul East

Printed and bound in the UK.
The Publisher's policy is to use paper manufactured from sustainable forests.

All photographs supplied by Alamy Images.
p8 David Millichope; p10 Jon Bower; p12 David Noble Photography; p15 europhotos;
p17 mediacolor's; p23 Stockfolio; p27 Chuck Pefley; p30 Jack Sullivan; p32 CW Images;
p35 Peter Bowater; p40 images-of-france; p43 Nick Hanna; p44 Hemis; p46 Simon
Grosset; p50 Lourens Smak; p57 travelstock44; p60 Art Kowalsky; p62 David Noton
Photography; p64 images-of-france; p68 Directphoto.org; p70 Eddie Linssen; p74 Hemis;
p75 Directphoto.org; p78 Images Etc Ltd; p84 Directphoto.org; p87 imagebroker; p90
foodfolio; p92 CW Images; p96 Agence Images; p100 Michele Molinari; p101 Martin
Beddall; p102 Robert Harding Picture Library Ltd; p104 Clynt Garnham; p109 Hemis;
p111 David Noble Photography; p116 Iksung Nah; p120 SAS; p124 Sébastien Baussais;
p126 David Noton Photography.

Contents

Get By in French is divided into colour-coded topics to help you find what you need quickly. Each unit contains practical travel tips to help you get around and understand the country, and a phrasemaker, to help you say what you need to and understand what you hear.

As well as listing key phrases, Get By in French aims to help you understand how the language works so that you can build your own phrases and start to communicate independently. The check out dialogues within each section show the language in action, and the try it out exercises give you an opportunity to practise for yourself. The linkup sections pick out the key structures and give helpful notes about their use. A round-up of all the basic grammar can be found in the Language Builder, pp131-137.

In French, all nouns (things, people or concepts) are either masculine or feminine and this affects the way they are written and pronounced as well as the words related to them. In the book these alternative endings are shown as masculine/feminine, e.g. infirmier/infirmière, meaning male nurse/female nurse, or with the extra letter needed for the feminine ending in brackets, e.g. anglais(e), used to describe an English man (anglais) or an English woman (anglaise).

If you've bought the pack with the audio CD, you'll be able to listen to a selection of the most important phrases and check out dialogues, as well as all the as if you were there activities. You can use the book on its own, but the CD will help you improve your pronunciation.

sounds French

This book uses a pronunciation guide based on sounds you already know, to help you start speaking French. Key pronunciation points to remember are also highlighted in the sound checks throughout the units. French words are pronounced with almost equal stress on every syllable.

consonants

Consonants at the ends of words are not normally pronounced, except when followed by another word beginning with a vowel. So vous is normally pronounced *voo*, but vous avez would become *vooz avay*.

	sounds like …	shown as …
b	'b' in 'but'	*b*
c (+ **e** or **i**, also **ç**)	's' in 'sat'	*s*
c (otherwise)	'k' in 'kit'	*k*
ch	'sh' in 'shut'	*sh*
d	'd' in 'dog'	*d*
f	'f' in 'feet'	*f*
g (+**e** or **i**)	's' in 'measure'	*j*
gn	'ni' in 'onion'	*ny*
g (otherwise)	'g' in 'got'	*g*
h	always silent	
j	's' in 'measure'	*j*
k	'k' in 'kit'	*k*
l	'l' in 'look'	*l*
ll	'y' in 'yet'	*y*
m	'm' in 'mat'	*m*
n (see also nasal vowels)	'n' in 'not'	*n*
p (followed by **h**)	'f' in 'fast'	*f*
p (otherwise)	'p' in 'pack'	*p*
qu	'k' in 'kit'	*k*
r	rolled at back of throat	*r*
s (between vowels)	'z' in 'zoo'	*z*
s (otherwise)	's' in 'set'	*s*
t	't' in 'tin'	*t*
(note that the English 'th' sound doesn't exist in French; th is always t)		
v	'v' in 'vet'	*v*
w (except in words borrowed from English)	'v' in 'vet'	*v*
x (at end of words)	's' in 'say'	*s*
x (otherwise)	'x' in 'box'	*x*
y	'y' in 'yet'	*y*
z	'z' in 'zoo'	*z*

vowels

The pronunciation of vowels is often affected if:
- there's a written accent. E.g. it's escalier *eskalyay*, but épicerie *aypeesree*.
- they're followed by an **n** or **m** – these vowels usually have a nasal sound (try speaking through your nose and mouth at the same time). The **n** or **m** itself is not pronounced.
- they're in a combination of vowels (see next page).

	sounds like …	shown as …
a, **à**, **â**	between 'a' in 'cat' and 'cart'	*a*
é, **er**, **ez** (at end of word)	'a' in 'gate', but a bit shorter	*ay*
e, **è**, **ê**	'e' in 'get'	*e*
e (at end of word)	not pronounced	
e (at end of syllable or in one-syllable word)	often pronounced weakly, like 'er' in 'other'	*uh*
i	'ee' in 'meet'	*ee*
'weak' **i**	'y' in 'yet'	*y*
o	'o' in 'lot'	*o*
ô	'o' in 'note'	*oh*
u	shape your lips to say 'oo', then say 'ee'	*ew*

vowel combinations

	sounds like …	shown as …
ai	'a' in 'gate'	*ay*
aî	'e' in 'get'	*e*
ail	'i' in 'bite'	*iy*
au, **eau**	'o' in 'note'	*oh*
ei	'e' in 'get'	*e*
eu, **œu**	'er' in 'other'	*uh*
oi	'wa' in 'swam'	*wa*
ou, **oue**	'ou' in 'through'	*oo*
oy	'why'	*wiy*
ui	'wee' in 'between'	*wee*

nasal vowels

	sounds like …	shown as …
an, **en**, **em**	'o' in 'lot' + nasal sound	*oñ*
ain, **ein**, **in**	'a' in 'cat' + nasal sound	*añ*
on	'aw' in 'saw' + nasal sound	*awñ*
un	'u' in 'cut' + nasal sound	*uñ*

pronouncing the alphabet

A *a*	**B** *bay*	**C** *say*	**D** *day*	**E** *uh*	**F** *ef*	**G** *jay*
H *ash*	**I** *ee*	**J** *jee*	**K** *ka*	**L** *el*	**M** *em*	**N** *en*
O *oh*	**P** *pay*	**Q** *kew*	**R** *er*	**S** *es*	**T** *tay*	**U** *ew*
V *vay*	**W** *doo bluh vay*	**X** *eex*	**Y** *ee grekw*	**Z** *zed*		

Bare **Necessities**

greetings

you may say ...

Good morning!/		
Good afternoon!	Bonjour ...	*bawñjoor*
(to a man)	Monsieur!	*muhsyuh*
(to a woman)	Madame!	*madam*
(to a young girl)	Mademoiselle!	*madmwazel*
Good evening!	Bonsoir!	*bawñswar*
Good night.	Bonne nuit.	*bon nwee*
Hi!/Bye! (informal)	Salut!	*salew*
How are you?	Comment allez-vous?	*komoñt alay voo*
How are things?	Comment ça va?	*komoñ sa va*
Fine, and you?	Ça va, et vous?	*sa va ay voo*
See you later! (the same day)	À tout à l'heure!	*a toot a luhr*
See you tomorrow!	À demain!	*a duhmañ*
goodbye	au revoir	*oh ruhvwar*

other useful words

you may say ...

excuse me	excusez-moi	*exkewzay mwa*
please	s'il vous plaît	*seelvooplay*
Thank you (very much).	Merci (beaucoup).	*mersee (bohkoo)*
You're very kind.	Vous êtes très aimable.	*vooz et trez aymabl*
You're welcome.	De rien.	*duh ryañ*
I'm sorry.	Je suis désolé(e).	*juh swee dayzohlay*
yes/no	oui/non	*wee/nawñ*
okay	OK/d'accord	*ohkay/dakor*
No, thank you.	Non, merci.	*nawñ mersee*

asking where things are

you may say …

Is there a lift?	Il y a un ascenseur?	*eelya uñ nasoñsuhr*
Are there any toilets?	Il y a des toilettes?	*eelya day twalet*
Where is …	Où est …	*oo ay*
the town centre?	le centre-ville?	*luh soñtr veel*
the station?	la gare?	*la gar*
Where are …	Où sont …	*oo sawñ*
the shoes?	les chaussures?	*lay shohsewr*
the newspapers?	les journaux?	*lay joornoh*

you may hear …

C'est à droite/ à gauche.	*sayt a drwat/ a gohsh*	It's on the right/ on the left.

do you have any …?

you may say …

Do you have any …	Avez-vous …	*avay voo*
sandwiches?	des sandwichs?	*day soñdweetsh*
cheese?	du fromage?	*dew fromaj*

how much ...?

you may say ...

How much?/ How many?	Combien?	*kawñbyañ*
How much is that?	Ça fait combien?	*sa fay kawñbyañ*

I'd like ...

you may say ...

I'd like ...	Je voudrais ...	*juh voodray*
a T-shirt.	un tee-shirt.	*uñ teeshuhrt*
a melon.	un melon.	*uñ muhlawñ*
I'd like a kilo of ...	Je voudrais un kilo de ...	*juh voodray uñ keeloh duh*
apples.	pommes.	*pom*
carrots.	carrottes.	*karot*

you may hear ...

Autre chose?	*ohtr shohz*	**Anything else?**

getting things straight

you may say ...

Pardon?	Comment?	*komoñ*
Could you ...	Vous pouvez	*voo poovay*
say that again?	répéter?	*raypaytay*
write it down?	l'écrire?	*laykreer*
speak more slowly?	parler plus lentement?	*parlay plew loñtuhmoñ*
I don't understand.	Je ne comprends pas.	*juh nuh kawñproñ pa*
I understand.	Je comprends.	*juh kawñproñ*
Do you speak English?	Vous parlez anglais?	*voo parlay oñglay*

check out 1

You're shopping in a small village grocer's.

○ Où sont les tomates, s'il vous plaît?
oo sawñ lay tomat seelvooplay

- Là-bas, Monsieur ... Autre chose?
laba muhsyuh ... ohtr shohz

○ Oui, avez-vous un journal en anglais?
wee avay vooz uñ joornal oñ noñglay

- Oui, ils sont à droite, là.
wee eel sawñ ta drwat la

○ Merci, c'est tout. Ça fait combien?
mersee say too. sa fay kawñbyañ

- Ça fait trois euros soixante-dix, s'il vous plaît.
sa fay trwaz uhroh swasoñt dees seelvooplay

(là-bas = over there)

Q Are the English newspapers on the right or the left?
What is the total cost?

4

talking about yourself & others

you may say ...

My name is ...	Je m'appelle ...	*juh mapel*
I'm ...	Je suis ...	*juh swee(z)*
English.	anglais(e).	*oñglay/oñglez*
Irish.	irlandais(e).	*eerloñday/eerloñdez*
(See p16 for more nationalities.)		
I'm from Glasgow.	Je suis de Glasgow.	*juh swee duh glazgoh*
I'm 33 (years old).	J'ai trente-trois ans.	*jay troñt trwaz oñ*
I'm ...	Je suis ...	*juh swee .*
single.	célibataire.	*sayleebater*
married.	marié(e).	*maryay*
divorced.	divorcé(e).	*deevorsay*
a widow/widower.	veuf/veuve.	*vuhf/vuhv*
I have two children.	J'ai deux enfants.	*jay duhz oñfoñ*
I'm a ...	Je suis ...	*juh swee(z)*
student.	étudiant(e)	*aytewdyoñ(t)*
lawyer.	avocat(e).	*àvohka(t)*
teacher.	professeur.	*profesuhr*
nurse.	infirmier/	*añfeermyay/*
	infirmière.	*añfeermyer*
I work in ...	Je travaille dans ...	*juh traviy doñ(z)*
an office.	un bureau.	*uñ bewroh*
a shop.	un magasin.	*uñ magazañ*
I'm on holiday here.	Je suis en vacances ici.	*juh sweez oñ vakoñs eesee*
I'm here on business.	Je suis ici pour affaires.	*juh sweez eesee poor afer*
I speak a little French.	Je parle un peu français.	*juh parl uñ puh froñsay*

(For the alphabet and how to spell your name, see p6.)

you may hear ...

Comment vous appelez-vous?	*komoñ vooz aplay voo*	What's your name?
Je vous présente ...	*juh voo prayzoñt*	May I introduce ...
ma femme.	*ma fam*	my wife?
mon mari.	*mawñ maree*	my husband?
mon compagnon/ ma compagne.	*mawñ kawñpanyawñl ma kawñpany*	my partner?
Enchanté(e)!	*oñshoñtay*	Pleased to meet you.
Vous êtes d'où?	*vooz et doo*	Where are you from?
Vous venez d'où?	*voo vuhnay doo*	Where do you come from?
Qu'est-ce que vous faites (comme travail)?	*keskuh voo fet (com traviy)*	What do you do (for a living)?
Vous êtes en vacances?	*vooz et oñ vakoñs*	Are you on holiday?
Vous voulez ...	*voo voolay*	Would you like ...
prendre un verre?	*proñdr uñ ver*	to go for a drink?

the time

you may say ...

What time is it?	Quelle heure est-il?	*kel uhr ayteel*
What time does ...	... à quelle heure?	*... a kel uhr*
the train leave/ arrive?	Le train part/arrive	*luh trañ par/areev*
the shop open/ close?	Le magasin ouvre/ ferme	*luh magazañ oovrl ferm*

check out 2

You get chatting to the owner of a gift shop.

○ Bonjour, Monsieur. Comment allez-vous?
bawñjoor muhsyuh. komoñt alay voo

- Bonjour, Madame, bien, et vous?
bawñjoor madam byañ ay voo

○ Bien, merci. Vous parlez bien français!
byañ mersee. voo parlay byañ froñsay

- Merci, je parle français souvent au travail.
mersee juh parl froñsay soovoñ oh traviy

○ Qu'est-ce que vous faites?
keskuh voo fet

- Je travaille dans une banque internationale,
à Londres, mais je suis d'Édimbourg.
*juh traviy doñz ewn boñk añternasyonal
a lawñdr, may juh swee dedañboor*

(souvent = often)

Q What does the shop owner say about your French?
What two questions are you asked?

you may hear ...

Il est quatorze heures trente.	*eel ay katorz uhr troñt*	It's 14.30.
dans cinq minutes/ trois heures	*doñ sañk meenewt/ trwaz uhr*	in five minutes/ three hours
Il est une heure et quart/et demie.	*eel ay ewn uhr ay kar/ay duhmee*	It's quarter/half past one.
pas avant cinq heures (moins vingt)	*paz avoñ sañk uhr (mwañ vañ)*	not until (twenty to) five
à partir de/jusqu'à dix heures	*a parteer duh/jewska deez uhr*	from/until ten o'clock
à midi/minuit	*a meedee/meenwee*	at noon/midnight

changing money

you may say ...

I'd like to change 50 pounds into euros.	Je voudrais changer cinquante livres en euros.	*juh voodray shoñjay sañkoñt leevr oñ nuhroh*
What is the exchange rate?	Quel est le taux de change?	*kel ay luh toh duh shoñj*
How much is the commission?	C'est combien, la commission?	*say kawñbyañ la komisyawñ*
a €20 note	un billet de vingt euros	*uñ beeyay duh vañt uhroh*
a €1 coin	une pièce d'un euro	*ewn pyes duñ nuhroh*

numbers

0	zéro	*zayroh*	22	vingt-deux		*vañtduh*
1	un	*uñ*	30	trente		*troñt*
2	deux	*duh*	31	trente et un		*troñtayuñ*
3	trois	*trwa*	40	quarante		*karoñt*
4	quatre	*katr*	50	cinquante		*sañkoñt*
5	cinq	*sañk*	60	soixante		*swasoñt*
6	six	*sees*	70	soixante-dix		*swasoñt dees*
7	sept	*set*	71	soixante et onze		*swasoñtayawñz*
8	huit	*weet*	72	soixante-douze		*swasoñt dooz*
9	neuf	*nuhf*	80	quatre-vingts		*katruhvañ*
10	dix	*dees*	81	quatre-vingt-un		*katruhvañ uñ*
11	onze	*awñz*	90	quatre-vingt-dix		*katruhvañ dees*
12	douze	*dooz*	91	quatre-vingt-onze		*katruhvañ awñz*
13	treize	*trez*	100	cent		*soñ*
14	quatorze	*katorz*	101	cent un		*soñ uñ*
15	quinze	*kañz*	102	cent deux		*soñ duh*
16	seize	*sez*	200	deux cents		*duh soñ*
17	dix-sept	*deeset*	2000	deux mille		*duh meel*
18	dix-huit	*deezweet*	1st	premier		*pruhmyay*
19	dix-neuf	*deeznuhf*	2nd	deuxième		*duhzyem*
20	vingt	*vañ*	3rd	troisième		*trwazyem*
21	vingt et un	*vañtayuñ*				

check out 3

You're at the bank to get some euros.

○ Bonjour.
  bawñjoor

- Bonjour, Mademoiselle. Je voudrais changer
  quarante livres en euros, s'il vous plaît.
  bawñjoor madmwazel juh voodray shoñjay
  karoñt leevr oñ nuhroh seelvooplay

○ Oui, le taux de change est à un euro quarante.
  La commission est de cinq euros.
  wee luh toh duh shoñj ayt a uñ nuhroh karoñt.
  la komisyawñ ay duh sañk uhroh

- D'accord.
  dakor

○ Voilà, cinquante et un euros.
  vwala sañkoñtayuñ nuhroh

Q You want to change £14 into euros: true or false?
What is the exchange rate?

countries & nationalities

Australia: Australian	l'Australie (f): australien/ australienne	*lohstralee: ohstralyañ/ ohstralyen*
Belgium: Belgian	la Belgique: belge	*la beljeek: belj*
Canada: Canadian	le Canada: canadien/canadienne	*luh kanada: kanadyañ/kanadyen*
England: English	l'Angleterre (f): anglais/anglaise	*loñgluhter: oñglay/oñglez*
France: French	la France: français/française	*la froñs: froñsay/froñsez*
Germany: German	l'Allemagne (f): allemand/allemande	*lalmany: almoñ/almoñd*
Great Britain: British	la Grande-Bretagne: britannique	*la groñd bruhtany: breetaneek*
Ireland: Irish	l'Irlande (f): irlandais/irlandaise	*leerloñd: eerloñday/eerloñdez*
Luxembourg: Luxemburger	le Luxembourg: luxembourgeois(e)	*luh lewxoñboor: lewxoñboorjwa(z)*
New Zealand: New Zealander	la Nouvelle-Zélande: néo-Zélandais/ néo-Zélandaise	*la noovelzayloñd: nayohzayloñday/ nayohzayloñdez*
Northern Ireland: Northern Irish	l'Irlande du Nord (f): irlandais/ irlandaise	*leerloñd dew nor: eerloñday/ eerlawñdez*
Scotland: Scottish	l'Écosse (f): écossais/écossaise	*laykos: aykosay/aykosez*
South Africa: South African	l'Afrique du Sud (f): sud-Africain/ sud-Africaine	*lafreek dew sewd: sewd afreekañ/ sewd afreeken*
Spain: Spanish	l'Espagne (f): espagnol(e)	*lespany: espanyol*
Switzerland: Swiss	la Suisse: suisse	*la swees: swees*
United States: American	les Etats-Unis (mpl): américain/ américaine	*layz aytaz ewnee: amayreekañ/ amayreeken*
Wales: Welsh	le Pays de Galles: gallois(e)	*luh payy duh gal: galwa(z)*

days

Monday	lundi	*luñdee*
Tuesday	mardi	*mardee*
Wednesday	mercredi	*mercruhdee*
Thursday	jeudi	*juhdee*
Friday	vendredi	*voñdruhdee*
Saturday	samedi	*samdee*
Sunday	dimanche	*deemoñsh*

months

January	janvier	*joñvyay*
February	février	*fayvreeyay*
March	mars	*mars*
April	avril	*avreel*
May	mai	*may*
June	juin	*jwañ*
July	juillet	*jweeye*
August	août	*oot*
September	septembre	*septoñbr*
October	octobre	*octobr*
November	novembre	*novoñbr*
December	décembre	*daysoñbr*

c is pronounced in two ways, depending on the letter that follows it.

ç, **ce**, or **ci** – like the 's' in 'sat':
ça va *sa va*   cent *soñ*
c otherwise sounds like the 'k' in 'kit':
comment *komoñ*   d'accord *dakor*
Practise on these words:
célibataire *sayleebater*   ceinture *sañtewr*
commission *komisyawñ*   vacances *vakoñs*

try it out

know-how
How might you:

1 wish someone good night and say you'll see them tomorrow?
2 tell someone you're Welsh, from Cardiff?
3 invite someone for a drink?
4 say you're 45 and have three children?

match it up
Match the questions with the correct answers.

1 Comment ça va?   **a** Je parle un peu anglais.
2 D'où êtes-vous?   **b** Ça va, et vous?
3 Vous parlez anglais?   **c** Ça fait quatre euros trente-trois.
4 À quelle heure part le train?   **d** Je suis de Paris.
5 Ça fait combien?   **e** Je ne travaille pas, je suis étudiante.
6 Qu'est-ce que vous faites comme travail?   **f** À dix heures vingt-cinq.

time flies ...

Add 15 minutes to each of the following times,
and write out your answer in full.

1 Il est deux heures et demie.
2 Le magasin ferme à dix-neuf heures.
3 Le train va partir dans dix minutes.
4 Jusqu'à midi.
5 Ma femme arrive à dix heures moins cinq.

as if you were there

Imagine you're on holiday, and a local man strikes up a
conversation with you. Follow the prompts to play your
part.

Bonjour, comment allez-vous?
(Say good afternoon, you're well, thank you, and ask after him)
Ça va, merci. Vous êtes en vacances?
(Say yes, you're from London)
Je m'appelle Paul. Et vous?
(Say your name is Katherine)
Enchanté, Katherine. Au revoir.

linkup

key phrases		
	Je m'appelle ...	**My name is ...**
	Je suis anglais(e).	**I'm** English.
	Je viens de Manchester.	**I come from** Manchester.
	J'ai deux enfants.	**I have** two children.
	Où est la gare?	**Where's** the station?
	Il y a un bar/ des toilettes?	**Is there** a bar?/ **Are there** any toilets?
	Vous avez des pommes?	**Do you have** any apples?
	Je voudrais de la limonade.	**I'd like** some lemonade.
	Pouvez-vous parler plus lentement?	**Can you** speak more slowly?

listening & replying

When people ask you questions about yourself, such as
Vous venez d'où? (Where do you come from?), it's tempting to
reply using the word you've just heard: venez.

In French, however, the word for 'come', like all verbs, changes
depending on who's doing the action. So, it's Je **viens** de
(I come from), not **venez**, which is the vous form.

Notice the different verb forms in these common questions and
answers:
Vous **avez** des enfants? – Oui, j'**ai** deux garçons.
Do you have any children? – Yes, I have two boys.
Vous **êtes** anglais(e)? – Non, je **suis** irlandais(e).
Are you English? – No, I'm Irish.

For more on verbs, see the Language Builder, p136. ····>

different ways of saying things

You often say things differently in French than in English, so you can't always translate word for word. To say 'My name is Claire', for example, use Je m'appelle Claire (literally, I call myself Claire).

Another example is the French use of the verb 'have' where we would say 'am' or 'are':

J'ai trente ans. I'm 30. (literally, I have 30 years)
Vous avez froid/chaud? Are you cold/hot? (literally, Do you have cold/hot?)

It is often worth learning the whole phrase, not just the individual words.

addressing people

The French are extremely polite. The meeting and greeting process involves much kissing and shaking of hands, and you'll often hear – and should use yourself – the titles Monsieur, Madame and Mademoiselle.

Some phrases you may say are:
Bonjour, Monsieur. Good morning./Good afternoon. (to a man)
De rien, Madame. You're welcome. (to a woman)
Excusez-moi, Mademoiselle. Excuse me. (to a young woman)

Getting **Around**

driving in France

French roads seem large and empty by European standards, and drivers are well-catered for. Take care though, as accident statistics are alarming. On town and country roads, unmarked T-junctions have **priorité à droite** (give way to the right). Roundabout etiquette is seldom observed and people rarely indicate. The police carry out random **contrôles de vitesse** (speed checks), so don't worry if oncoming drivers flash their lights – they are probably warning of a radar or road check ahead! There are moves towards stricter enforcement of drink-driving legislation and you may be asked to take an **alcootest** (breath test). For a long journey, you can take your car on the train.

International car hire companies have desks in airports and major train stations. Check for distance restrictions – ask for **kilométrage illimité** (unlimited kilometres) if in doubt. Pay any fines to your hirer, who will deal with the paperwork.

Petrol Although fuel prices are on the rise in France, as elsewhere, **gasoil/gazole** (diesel) remains relatively cheap and is available everywhere, as is **sans plomb** (unleaded). Supermarket service stations often have automatic 24-hour pumps with Visa/Mastercard payment; smaller garages tend to close on Sundays and early evenings; remote regions can be quite 'dry'.

Travelling at peak times is to be avoided, where possible! French regions stagger school holidays to relieve traffic pressure, but motorways out of major cities are always blocked on the main national holidays. Look out for warnings of **bouchons** (tailbacks). Precise dates vary; black spots are late October to early November, Christmas and New Year, February, Easter week, Pentecost (late May), early to mid-July and 15th–30th August (when the entire country tends to take a summer break).

Les autoroutes Motorways are mostly numbered clockwise around Paris, starting with the A1, which runs north. They are free around major cities, after which **le péage** (toll system) operates. Collect a ticket and pay at the next toll. Larger **péages** have manned and automated lanes (Visa/Mastercard), cash-only and subscribers' lanes. Motorway driving is fast, often with only two lanes in each direction, and frequent **aires de repos** (rest areas), which often have children's play areas. Look out too for brown signs indicating local sights.

Les nationales The national N-roads, also numbered clockwise from Paris, are fine for touring but frustrating if you're in a hurry; they are often jammed through town centres (ring roads – **rocade** or **boulevard périphérique** – are still relatively rare).

Les départementales Often quiet and attractive roads, D-road numbers change between **départements**. All numbers are marked on the top of signposts and on yellow-and-white **bornes** (roadside kilometre markers).

Chemins communaux C-roads are small country and village lanes.

taking the train

All railway stations are signposted **Gare SNCF**. France's famous high-speed train, the TGV, connects Paris with European and regional cities. TGV trains have couchettes and access for wheelchair users.

To book seats on **grandes lignes** (mainline services) look for the 'i' sign in large stations. Local tickets can be bought from a **billeterie automatique** (ticket machine) or **au guichet** (at the ticket office). Be aware that for certain trains reservation is compulsory, and you must stamp your ticket at the platform machines or face a fine. There are a number of **réductions/tarifs spéciaux** (special fares) available for young people, students, seniors, couples and families – ask for advice before you buy. Note also that it's always cheaper to travel off-peak (**période bleue**, as opposed to the times designated **blanc** or **rouge**). For timetables and booking see **www.raileurope. co.uk**. There's also an English version of the SNCF website: **www.sncf.fr**.

coaches & buses

Travel between neighbouring towns can be more convenient by coach than train – ask about **correspondances autocar** (coach connections).

Local bus services run from the **gare routière** (central bus station) in all main towns. Town centres and suburbs tend to be well-served, rural areas sometimes not at all, or only around school times (7.30am and 5pm). Tickets can usually be bought on the bus itself, at the ticket office (in larger bus stations), or sometimes at a **tabac** (tobacconist's). A **carnet** (book of ten tickets) may be cheaper for frequent local trips. Remember to stamp your ticket if there is a machine on board.

internal flights

Major regional airports have competitively-priced frequent shuttle services to Paris (mostly Orly). Air Inter, the state domestic airline, no longer has a monopoly, so shop around (try TAT and AOM). You can buy tickets on the spot, with the usual discounts for young people, off-peak travel, etc.

boating

Popular options include the Canal du Midi (from Toulouse to the Mediterranean at Agde), and the system linking St-Malo, Nantes and Rennes in Brittany.

phrasemaker

asking the way

you may say …

Excuse me (to a man/woman).	Pardon (Monsieur/Madame).	*pardawñ (muhsyuh/madam)*
Which way is …	Pour aller …	*poor alay*
the station?	à la gare?	*a la gar*
the town centre?	au centre-ville?	*oh soñtr veel*
the post office?	à la poste?	*a la post*
Is it (very) far?	C'est (très) loin?	*say (tre) lwañ*
Is/Are there … near here?	Il y a … près d'ici?	*eelya … pre deesee*
a park	un jardin public	*uñ jardañ pewbleek*
toilets	des toilettes	*day twalet*
a taxi rank	une station de taxis	*ewn stasyawñ duh taxee*
a cashpoint	un distributeur automatique de billets	*uñ deestreebewtuhr ohtomateek duh beeyay*
Is this the right way to …	C'est le chemin …	*say luh shumañ*
the castle?	du château?	*dew shatoh*
the museum?	du musée?	*dew mewzay*
the airport?	de l'aéroport?	*duh laayropor*
the port?	du port?	*dew por*
I'm looking for …	Je cherche …	*juh shersh*
the bus station.	la gare d'autobus.	*la gar dohtohbews*
the coach station.	la gare routière.	*la gar rootyer*
an internet café.	un cybercafé.	*uñ seeberkafay*
Where's the nearest …	Où est … le/la plus proche?	*oo ay … luh/la plew prosh*
pedestrian crossing?	le passage clouté	*le pasaj klootay*
petrol station?	la station-service/ la station d'essence	*la stasyawñ servees/ la stasyawñ desoñs*
I'm lost.	Je suis perdu(e).	*juh swee perdew*
Is it wheelchair-friendly?	C'est accessible aux fauteuils roulants?	*say axeseebluh oh fohtuhy rooloñ*

you may hear ...

C'est là!	*say la*	There it is!
Tournez (à droite/à gauche) aux feux rouges.	*toornay (a drwat/a gohsh) oh fuh rooj*	Turn (right/left) at the traffic lights.
c'est à droite/ à gauche	*sayt a drwat/ a gohsh*	it's on the right/ on the left
traversez la rue/ la place	*traversay la rew/ la plas*	cross the street/ the square
(allez/continuez) tout droit	*alay/kawñteeneway too drwa*	(go/keep going) straight on
passez le pont	*pasay luh pawñ*	cross the bridge
prenez ...	*pruhnay*	take ...
la première rue à droite	*la pruhmyer rew a drwat*	the first street on the right
la deuxième rue à gauche	*la duhzyem rew a gohsh*	the second street on the left
jusqu' ...	*jewskoh*	as far as ...
au rond-point	*rawñpwañ*	the roundabout
aux remparts	*roñpar*	the city walls
C'est à (environ) cent mètres.	*sayt a (oñveerawñ) soñ metr*	It's (about) 100 metres away.
C'est une rue piétonne.	*sayt ewn rew pyayton*	It's a pedestrian street.
au bout de la rue	*oh boo duh la rew*	at the end of the street
C'est au coin.	*sayt oh kwañ*	It's on the corner.
c'est ...	*say(t)*	it's ...
(assez) près	*(asay) pre*	(quite) near
en face de	*oñ fas duh*	opposite
devant	*devoñ*	in front of
derrière	*deryer*	behind
à côté de	*a kohtay duh*	next to

(See p60 for a list of French shops, and p104 for places you may want to visit.)

check out 1

You stop a passer-by to ask for directions.

○ Pardon, Madame, il y a une pharmacie près d'ici, s'il vous plaît?

pardawñ madam eelya ewn farmasee pre deesee seelvooplay

- Oui. Allez tout droit, jusqu'aux feux, traversez la rue, continuez et prenez la première rue à droite.

wee. alay too drwa jewskoh fuh traversay la rew kawñteeneway ay pruhnay la pruhmyer rew a drwat

○ Merci beaucoup.

mersee bohkoo

Q You are told to take the second road on the right: true or false?

hiring a car or bike

you may say ...

I'd like to hire ...	Je voudrais louer ...	*juh voodray looay*
a small/	une petite/	*ewn puhteet/*
large car.	grande voiture.	*gronrd vwatewr*
a three/five-door car.	une voiture à trois/ cinq portes.	*ewn vwatewr a trwa/ sañk port*
a motorbike.	une moto.	*ewn moto*
a bike.	un vélo.	*uñ vayloh*
for ...	pour ...	*poor*
two days	deux jours	*duh joor*
a week	une semaine	*ewn suhmen*
How much is it per day/per week?	C'est combien par jour/par semaine?	*say kawñbyañ par joor/par suhmen*
Is it unlimited mileage?	C'est kilométrage illimité?	*say keelohmaytraj eeleemeetay*
Is insurance included?	L'assurance est comprise?	*lasewronrs ay kawñpreez*

you may hear...

Pour combien de jours?	*poor kawñbyañ duh joor*	For how many days?
Qui va conduire?	*kee va kawñdweer*	Who'll be driving?
Votre permis/ passeport, s'il vous plaît.	*votr permee/ paspor seelvooplay*	Your driving licence/ passport, please.
Il y a une caution à payer.	*eelya ewn kohsyawñ a payyay*	There's a deposit to pay.

check out 2

You want to hire a small car for your holiday.

○ Bonjour. Je voudrais louer une petite voiture.
C'est combien par jour?
bawñjoor juh voodray looay ewn puhteet vwatewr.
say kawñbyañ par joor

- Nous avons une très belle voiture à trois portes,
soixante euros par jour.
nooz avawñ ewn tre bel vwatewr a trwa port
swasoñt uhroh par joor

○ C'est kilométrage illimité?
say keelohmaytraj eeleemeetay

- Oui, et l'assurance est comprise. Votre permis de
conduire, s'il vous plaît?
wee ay lasewroñs ay kawñpreez. votr permee duh
kawñdweer seelvooplay

(très belle = very nice)

Q What does the assistant say is included?
What does she ask to see?

buying petrol

you may say ...

30 litres of ...	trente litres de ...	*troñt leetr duh*
unleaded/	sans plomb/	*soñ plawñ/*
diesel/4-star	gasoil/super	*gazwal/sewper*
Which pump is it?	C'est quelle pompe?	*say kel pomp*
Have you got any ...	Vous avez ...	*vooz avay*
air?	de l'air?	*duh ler*
water?	de l'eau?	*duh loh*
oil?	de l'huile?	*duh lweel*
maps?	des cartes?	*day kart*
How much is it?	Ça fait combien?	*sa fay kawñbyañ*

on the road

Is this the right way to Dijon?	C'est bien la route de Dijon?	*say byañ la root duh deejawñ*
How many kilometres to ...?	... est à combien de kilomètres?	*... ayt a kawñbyañ duh keelohmetr*
Is Bordeaux far (from here)?	Bordeaux est loin (d'ici)?	*bordoh ay lwañ (deesee)*
Can I park here?	Je peux stationner ici?	*juh puh stasyonay eesee*
Where is the car park?	Où est le parking?	*oo ay luh parkeeng*

road signs

cédez le passage	give way
gravillons	loose chippings
impasse	no through road
passage protégé	right of way
poids lourds	heavy goods vehicles
ralentir	slow down
sens unique	one-way
serrez à droite	keep to the right
sortie	exit
stationnement interdit	no parking

Getting **Around**

taking a taxi

To ... please.	À ... s'il vous plaît.	a ... seelvooplay
this address	cette adresse	set adres
the airport	l'aéroport	laayropor
Quickly, please!	Vite, s'il vous plaît!	veet seelvooplay
How long will it take?	Combien de temps ça prendra?	kawñbyañ duh toñ sa proñdra
How much will it cost?	Ça va coûter combien?	sa va kootay kawñbyañ
I'd like a receipt.	Je voudrais un reçu.	juh voodray uñ ruhsew

Ce n'est pas loin.	se nay pa lwañ	It's not far.
C'est assez loin.	sayt asay lwañ	It's quite a way.
Pas longtemps.	pa lawñtoñ	Not long.

using the metro

one ticket	un ticket	uñ teekay
book of tickets	un carnet	uñ karnay
special tourist ticket	un billet touriste	uñ beeyay tooreest
Does this train go to Paris?	Ce train va à Paris?	suh trañ va a paree
Which line do I need for Bastille?	Quelle ligne pour Bastille?	kel leenyuh poor basteey
Is the next stop Gare du Nord?	Le prochain arrêt, c'est bien Gare du Nord?	luh proshañ naray say byañ gar dew nor

Il faut changer à Étoile.	eel foh shoñjay a aytwal	You need to change at Étoile.
Prenez la ligne rouge.	pruhnay la leenyuh rooj	Take the red line.
Descendez à Châtelet.	desoñday a shatlay	Get off at Châtelet.

check out 3

You stop for petrol and to ask for directions.

○ Bonjour. C'est où, le sans plomb?
   bawñjoor. say oo luh soñ plawñ

- C'est là-bas, pompe numéro quatre.
   say laba pomp newmeroh katr

○ Merci. Et pour l'autoroute, c'est à combien de kilomètres?
   mersee. ay poor lohtohroot sayt a kawñbyañ duh keelohmetr

- Environ quinze kilomètres. Attention! Il y a un péage!
   oñveerawñ kañz keelohmetr. atoñsyawñ. eelya uñ payaj

Q What kind of petrol do you need?
   You're warned about some roadworks: true or false?

Getting **Around**

getting information about your journey

Are there any buses/ trains/coaches to ...?	Il y a des bus/trains/ cars pour ...?	*eelya day bews/trañ/ kar poor*
Is there a shuttle service to the airport?	Il y a une navette pour aller à l'aéroport?	*eelya ewn navet poor alay a laayropor*
What time does the ... leave/arrive?	... part/arrive à quelle heure?	*... par/areev a kel uhr*
bus	Le bus	*luh bews*
plane	L'avion	*lavyawñ*
boat	Le bateau	*luh batoh*
What number is it?	C'est quel numéro?	*say kel newmayroh*
Can I buy a ticket on the bus?	Je peux acheter un billet dans le bus?	*juh puh ashtay uñ beeyay doñ luh bews*
Where is the nearest bus/tram stop?	Où est l'arrêt de bus/tram le plus proche?	*oo ay laray duh bews/tram luh plew prosh*
What time does the (next/last) train leave?	À quelle heure part le (prochain/dernier) train?	*a kel uhr par luh (proshañ/dernyay) trañ*
Which platform?	Quel quai?	*kel kay*
Is there a lift?	Est-ce qu'il y a un ascenseur?	*eskeelya uñ asoñsuhr*
How long does ... take?	Ça prend combien de temps, ...?	*sa proñ kawñbyañ duh toñ ...*
the flight	le vol?	*luh vol*
the crossing	la traversée?	*la traversay*
the journey	le voyage?	*luh vwiyaj*
How long does it take?	Ça prend combien de temps?	*sa proñ kawñbyañ duh toñ*
Have you got a timetable?	Avez-vous un horaire?	*avay voo uñ norer*
Does it stop at ...?	Il s'arrête à ...?	*eel saret a*
Which stop should I get off at?	Je dois descendre à quel arrêt?	*juh dwa desoñdr a kel aray*
Where is the left-luggage office?	Où est la consigne?	*oo ay la kawñseeny*

Descendez à ...	*desoñday a*	Get off at ...
Il faut changer à ...	*eel foh shoñjay a*	You must change at ...
Il y a une correspondance.	*eelya ewn korespawñdoñs*	There's a connection.
Je vais vous montrer.	*juh vay voo mawñtray*	I'll show you.
Il faut faire l'appoint.	*eel foh fer lapwañ*	You have to give the exact money.

buying a ticket

Where's the ticket office?	Où est le guichet?	*oo ay luh geeshay*
a ... ticket to Paris return single	un ... pour Paris aller-retour aller simple	*uñ ... poor paree* *alay ruhtoor* *alay sañpl*
for two adults and one child	pour deux adultes et un enfant	*poor duhz adewlt ay uñ noñfoñ*
first/second class	première/deuxième classe	*pruhmyer/duhzyem klas*
I'd like to reserve ... a seat. a couchette.	Je voudrais réserver ... une place. une couchette.	*juh voodray rayzervay* *ewn plas* *ewn kooshet*
Is there a reduction for ... students? senior citizens?	Est-ce qu'il y a une réduction pour ... les étudiants? les personnes agées?	*eskeelya ewn raydewksyawñ poor* *layz aytewdyoñ* *lay personzajay*

Il y a un supplément de dix euros.	*eelya uñ sewplaymoñ duh dees uhroh*	There's a €10 supplement.
N'oubliez pas de composter.	*noobleeay pa duh kawñpostay*	Don't forget to validate your ticket.

Getting **Around**

check out 4

You're at the station to find out about trains to Saint-Tropez.

- Le prochain train pour St-Tropez part à quelle heure?
  luh proshañ trañ poor sañ trohpay par a kel uhr
- Quatorze heures vingt-huit. Il faut changer à Nice.
  katorz uhr vañtweet. eel foh shoñjay a nees
- Ça prend combien de temps?
  sa proñ kawñbyañ duh toñ
- Trois heures.
  trwaz uhr

Q Which of the following statements is true?
a) The train is direct.
b) The train leaves at 3pm.
c) The journey takes three hours.

sound check

Take care to distinguish between the sounds **oi**, **oy** and **ui**.
oi and **oy** are pronounced like the 'wa' in 'swam':

voiture *vwatewr*   droite *drwat*

voyage *vwayaj*

ui is pronounced like the 'wee' in 'between':

huile *weel*   conduire *kawñdweer*

Practise on these words:

trois *trwa*   voie *vwa*

noyer *nwiyay* **(to drown)** aboyer *abwiyay* **(to bark)**

fruit *frwee*   huit *weet*

try it out

picture this

Find the correct word or phrase to match each picture.

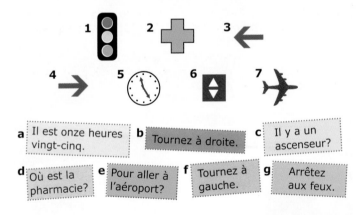

a Il est onze heures vingt-cinq.

b Tournez à droite.

c Il y a un ascenseur?

d Où est la pharmacie?

e Pour aller à l'aéroport?

f Tournez à gauche.

g Arrêtez aux feux.

Getting **Around**

mind the gap
Fill in the missing letters to make five French phrases.

1 You must change at Rouen: _ _ f_ _ _ changer à Rouen.

2 Cross the bridge: Passez le _ _ _t.

3 I'd like some diesel: Je v_ _ _ _ _ _ _ du g_ _ _ _ _.

4 Can I hire a bike?: Je p_ _x l_u _ _ un _ _ _o?

5 A single to Toulouse: Un a_ _ _ _ _ _m_ _e pour Toulouse, s'il vous plaît.

as if you were there
You need some petrol before finding the motorway. Follow the prompts below to play your part.

(Say excuse me and ask if there's a petrol station nearby)
Oui, c'est près du centre commercial. Continuez jusqu'au rond-point. C'est au coin, à gauche.
(Thank him and ask for directions to the motorway)
À cent mètres du centre commercial, passez le pont. Allez tout droit. L'autoroute se trouve là-bas.

linkup

Où est la piscine, s'il vous plaît?	**Where's** the swimming pool, please?
Où sont les toilettes, s'il vous plaît?	**Where are** the toilets please?
C'est loin?	**Is it** far?
Je cherche la mairie.	**I'm looking for** the town hall.
Il y a une station-service **près d'ici**?	**Is there** a petrol station **near here**?
Vous avez un plan de la ville?	**Do you have** a plan of the town?
Le train part **à quelle heure**?	**What time** does the train leave?
Je voudrais louer une voiture.	**I'd like** to hire a car.
Je peux stationner ici?	**Can I** park here?

asking questions

You can ask questions in different ways in French. Est-ce que turns any sentence into a question. It has no other meaning, so if you say it, you can be sure the French person you're talking to will know that you're asking a question.

Est-ce que vous avez un horaire? Do you have a timetable?

Another way – and probably the easiest – is simply to raise your intonation at the end of the sentence:

Vous avez un horaire? Do you have a timetable?

You can also form questions by changing the word order in a statement:

Avez-vous un horaire? Do you have a timetable?

Here are some more question words you'll find very handy:

Où? Where?
Comment? How?
Combien? How much?/How many?
Qui? Who?
Quand? When?
Que ...?/Qu'est-ce que ...? What?

For more on questions, see the Language Builder, p132. ·····⟩

saying where things are

Two very useful phrases when you're travelling around in France:

c'est loin it's far (away)
c'est près it's near

Use **de** with phrases describing where something is:

C'est en face de l'église. It's opposite the church.
C'est près de la poste. It's near the post office.
C'est juste à côté du musée. It's just next to the museum.

Notice the du in the last example. Du is used because musée is masculine, and de can't be followed by le; instead it becomes du.

For more on how **de** changes, see the Language Builder, p132. ·····⟩

When you're saying how far in time or distance, use **à**:

C'est à quinze kilomètres. It's 15km away.
C'est à cinq minutes. It's five minutes away.

Somewhere **to Stay**

The French like to holiday in France, so book ahead for busy school holidays: February to early March, May bank holidays, July to August, end of October to early November, Easter and Christmas. Local tourist offices have details of all types of accommodation.

hotels

French hotels range from grand châteaux to alpine chalets. Most are good value for money, particularly smaller family-run establishments. Hotels often have family rooms with double and single beds, and provide extra beds for a small charge. Room prices and facilities are listed on the back of each room's door and NN (**nouvelles normes**) star ratings range from zero to four. Look out for members of **Relais et Châteaux** (**www.relaischateaux. com**), **Demeures et Châteaux**, **Logis de France** (over 4,000 hotel-restaurants, 'chimney-piece' rating system) and **Relais du Silence** (quiet country hotels).

countryside holidays

Gîtes de France ('ear of corn' rating) offer a vast countrywide network of self-catering properties, **camping à la ferme** (farm camping), and **chambres d'hôtes** (B&Bs – sometimes serving dinner too). You can see detailed descriptions and book online at: **www.gîtes-de-france.fr**. They also offer properties geared to special-interest tourism, such as **Gîtes de Pêche** for anglers, **Gîtes et Cheval** for horseback treks, and **Gîtes Panda** for wildlife enthusiasts. Bed linen is not provided but can be hired. Look out too for **gîtes d'étape** and mountain refuges, providing dormitory rooms in remote areas.

For farm stay holidays, use **Bienvenue à la ferme** ('sunflower' rating), complete with farm tours, **les goûters à la ferme** (teas), **la chasse** (game shooting) and fresh produce: **www.bienvenue-a-la-ferme.com**. Try **les fermes-auberges** (farm restaurants offering home-cooked regional specialities), **les fermes équestres** (riding and trekking holidays, for all abilities), **les fermes de séjour** (half-board in an intimate setting) and **les campings en ferme d'accueil** (quiet campsites offering meals and trips).

An alternative network of self-catering properties is run by Clévacances: **www.clevacances.com**. Ask at tourist offices for details of other **locations saisonnières** (holiday lets).

campsites

Basic **campings municipaux** (municipal campsites) exist throughout France. Privately-run summer resorts rent tents, caravans and chalets, and often have electricity points for **les camping-cars** (motor-homes).

Aires naturelles de camping are the simplest of all sites. **Villages de vacances**, with individual chalets, are a popular alternative to camping. One of the best-known chains is Villages Vacances Familiales: **www.vvf-vacances.fr**.

phrasemaker

places to stay

bed and breakfast	la chambre d'hôte	*la shoñbr doht*
campsite	le terrain de camping	*luh terañ duh koñpeeng*
farmhouse	la ferme	*la ferm*
boarding house	la pension	*la poñsyawñ*
hotel	l'hôtel (m)	*lohtel*
rented room	la chambre louée	*la shoñbr looay*
self-catering flat	l'appartement (m)	*lapartuhmoñ*
self-catering cottage	le gîte meublé	*luh jeet muhblay*
youth hostel	l'auberge de jeunesse (f)	*lohberj duh juhnes*

finding a place

you may say …

Is there … near here?	Il y a … près d'ici?	*eelya … pre deesee*
a hotel	un hôtel	*uñ nohtel*
a campsite	un camping	*uñ koñpeeng*
Do you have a room available?	Vous avez une chambre de libre?	*vooz avay ewn shoñbr duh leebr*
I'd like a room for …	Je voudrais une chambre pour …	*juh voodray ewn shoñbr poor*
tonight.	ce soir.	*suh swar*
three nights.	trois nuits.	*trwa nwee*
four people.	quatre personnes.	*katr person*
two adults and two children.	deux adultes et deux enfants.	*duhz adewlt ay duhz oñfoñ*
a … room	une chambre …	*ewn shoñbr*
single	pour une personne	*poor ewn person*
double	double/à grand lit	*doobl/a groñ lee*
twin	à deux lits	*a duh lee*
family	de famille	*duh famee*
Can I see the room?	Je peux voir la chambre?	*juh puh vwar la shoñbr*
How much is it per night?	C'est combien par nuit?	*say kawñbyañ par nwee*

Somewhere **to Stay**

Do you have anything less expensive?	Vous en avez une moins cher?	*vooz oñ navay ewn mwañ sher*
Is there … a reduction for children? a single supplement?	Est-ce qu'il y a … une réduction pour les enfants? un supplément pour une chambre simple?	*eskeelya ewn raydewxyawñ poor layz oñfoñ uñ sewplaymoñ poor ewn shoñbr sañpl*
Can I book online?	Est-ce que je peux réserver en ligne?	*eskuh juh puh rayzervay oñ leeny*
I'll think about it.	Je vais réfléchir.	*juh vay rayflaysheer*
Okay, I'll take it.	D'accord, je la prends.	*dakor juh la proñ*

you may hear …

Pour combien de nuits?	*poor kawñbyañ duh nwee*	For how many nights?
Que voulez-vous comme chambre?	*kuh voolay voo kom shoñbr*	What sort of room do you want?
Pour combien de personnes?	*poor kawñbyañ duh person*	For how many people?
Désolé(e), c'est complet.	*dayzohlay say kawñple*	Sorry, we're full.
Demi-tarif pour les enfants.	*duhmee tareef poor layz oñfoñ*	Children are half price.
Demi-pension.	*duhmee poñsyawñ*	Half board.
Pension complète.	*poñsyawñ kawñplet*	Full board.

check out 1

You want to find out if a double room is available at a hotel.

○ Bonjour, Madame. Vous avez une chambre de libre?
bawñjoor madam. vooz avay ewn shoñbr duh leebr

- Oui, une chambre à grand lit et une chambre pour une personne.
wee ewn shoñbr a groñ lee ay ewn shoñbr poor ewn person

○ Je peux voir la chambre à grand lit?
C'est combien?
juh puh vwar la shoñbr a groñ lee
say kawñbyañ

- Soixante euros.
swasoñt uroh

○ Le petit déjeuner est compris?
luh puhtee dayjuhnay ay kawñpree

- Désolée, c'est en supplément.
dayzohlay sayt oñ sewplaymoñ

Q What types of room are available?
Breakfast is included: true or false? (clue: see p46)

Somewhere **to Stay**

specifications & services

you may say …

I'd like a room with a …	Je voudrais une chambre avec …	*juh voodray ewn shoñbr avek*
bathroom.	salle de bains.	*sal duh bañ*
shower.	douche.	*doosh*
bath.	baignoire.	*baynywar*
cot.	lit d'enfant.	*lee doñfoñ*
sink.	lavabo.	*lavaboh*
Could you add an extra bed?	Vous pouvez ajouter un autre lit?	*voo poovay ajootay uñ nohtr lee*
Is breakfast included?	Le petit déjeuner est compris?	*luh puhtee dayjuhnay ay kawñpree*
Do you have a room on the ground floor?	Vous avez une chambre au rez-de-chaussée?	*vooz avay ewn shoñbr oh ray duh shohsay*
Is the bathroom wheelchair-friendly?	La salle de bains est adaptée pour les fauteuils roulants?	*la sal duh bañ ayt adaptay poor lay fohtuhy rooloñ*
Is there …	Il y a …	*eelya*
a minibar?	un minibar?	*uñ meeneebar*
an iron?	un fer à repasser?	*uñ fer a ruhpasay*
room service?	un service en chambre?	*uñ servees oñ shoñbr*
an internet connection?	une connexion internet?	*ewn konexyawñ añternet*
What time is breakfast?	Le petit déjeuner est à quelle heure?	*luh puhtee dayjuhnay ayt a kel uhr*
I'd like breakfast in my room.	Je voudrais le petit déjeuner dans ma chambre.	*juh voodray luh puhtee dayjuhnay doñ ma shoñbr*
Where is the restaurant?	Où est le restaurant?	*oo ay luh restohroñ*
Is there …	Il y a …	*eelya*
a lift?	un ascenseur?	*uñ nasoñsuhr*
air-conditioning?	la climatisation?	*la kleemateezasyawñ*
Do you have a babysitting service?	Vous avez un service de garde d'enfants?	*vooz avay uñ servees duh gard doñfoñ*

45

you may hear ...

Le petit déjeuner est ...	*luh puhtee dayjuhnay ay*	Breakfast is ...
en supplement.	*toñ sewplaymoñ*	extra.
compris.	*kawñpree*	included.
Toutes taxes comprises/TTC.	*toot tax kawñpreez/ tay tay say*	All taxes are included.
Le petit déjeuner est de sept heures à huit heures et demie.	*luh puhtee dayjuhnay ay duh set uhr a weet uhr ay duhmee*	Breakfast is from 7am to 8.30am.
au ...	*oh*	on the ... floor
rez-de-chaussée	*ray duh shohsay*	ground
premier étage	*pruhmyay aytaj*	first
deuxième étage	*duhzyem aytaj*	second

checking in

you may say ...

I have a reservation.	J'ai une réservation.	*jay ewn rayzervasyawñ*
My name is ...	Mon nom est ...	*mawñ nawñ ay*
Where can I/we park?	Où peut-on stationner?	*oo puhtawñ stasyonay*

you may hear ...

Votre nom/passeport, s'il vous plaît.	*votr nawñ/paspor, seelvooplay*	Your name/passport, please.
Pourriez-vous remplir la fiche?	*pooryay voo roñpleer la feesh*	Could you fill in the form?
Quel est votre numéro d'immatriculation?	*kel ay votr newmayroh deematreekewlasyawñ*	What's your car's registration number?
Chambre vingt-quatre, au deuxième étage.	*shoñbr vañt katr oh duhzyem aytaj*	Room 24, on the second floor.

Somewhere **to Stay**

check out 2

You arrive at the hotel with a room reservation.

○ Bonjour, j'ai une réservation. Mon nom est King.
bawñjoor jay ewn rayzervasyawñ. mawñ nawñ ay king

- Ah oui, Monsieur King: une chambre à grand lit, avec salle de bains.
ah wee muhsyuh king ewn shoñbr a groñ lee avek sal duh bañ

○ Oui, c'est ça.
wee say sa

- Voilà, chambre douze, au premier étage. L'ascenseur est là-bas.
vwala shoñbr dooz oh pruhmyay aytaj. lasoñsuhr ay laba

○ Merci. Le petit déjeuner est à quelle heure?
mersee. luh puhtee dayjuhnay ayt a kel uhr

- À partir de six heures et demie. Il est servi dans le restaurant, au rez-de-chaussée.
a parteer duh seez uhr ay duhmee. eel ay servee doñ luh restohroñ oh ray duh shohsay

Q The room has a bathroom: true or false?
Where and when is breakfast served?

checking out
you may say ...

I'd like to pay the bill ...	Je voudrais payer ma note ...	*juh voodray payyay ma not*
with traveller's cheques.	avec des chèques de voyage.	*avek day shek duh vwiyaj*
by credit card.	avec une carte de crédit.	*avek ewn kart duh kraydee*
with cash.	en espèces.	*oñ nespes*
I think there's a mistake.	Je pense qu'il y a une erreur.	*juh poñs keelya ewn eruhr*

47

asking for help

Could I have an alarm call at ... ?	Vous pouvez me réveiller à ... ?	voo poovay muh rayvayay a
Have you got ...	Vous avez ...	vooz avay
a safe deposit box?	un coffre-fort?	uñ kofruhfor
a plan of the town?	un plan de la ville?	uñ ploñ duh la veel
Could you order me a taxi?	Vous pouvez m'appeler un taxi?	voo poovay mapuhlay uñ taxee
Could I have ...	Je peux avoir ...	juh puh avwar
a key?	une clé?	ewn klay
another towel?	une autre serviette?	ewn ohtr servyet
How do I get an outside number?	Comment obtenir une ligne extérieure?	komoñ obtuhneer ewn leeny extayreeyuhr
There's a problem with ...	Il y a un problème avec ...	eelya uñ problem avek
the shower.	la douche.	la doosh
the lighting.	la lumière.	la lewmyer
The ... isn't working.	... ne marche pas.	... nuh marsh pa
television	La télévision	la taylayveezyawñ
air conditioning	La climatisation	la kleemateezasyawñ
The room's ...	La chambre est ...	la shoñbr ay
very cold.	glacée.	glasay
too hot.	trop chaude.	tro shode
There's no ...	Il n'y a pas ...	eelnyapa
soap.	de savon.	duh savawñ
toilet paper.	de papier toilette.	duh papyay twalet
(hot) water.	d'eau (chaude).	doh (shohd)
There are no	Il n'y a pas ...	eelnyapa
hangers.	de cintres.	duh sañtr
blankets.	de couvertures.	duh koovertewr
It's very noisy.	C'est très bruyant.	say tre brweeyoñ

Je vais envoyer quelqu'un.	juh vay oñvwayay kelkuñ	I'll send somebody.
On vous en apporte.	awñ vooz oñ naport	We'll get you some.
Faites le zéro.	fet luh zayroh	Dial zero.

Somewhere **to Stay**

at the campsite

you may say ...

Do you have a pitch available for ...	Vous avez un emplacement de libre pour ...	*vooz avay uñ noñplasmoñ duh leebre poor*
a caravan?	une caravane?	*ewn karavan*
a tent?	une tente?	*ewn toñt*
How much is it per night?	C'est combien par nuit?	*say kawñbyañ par nwee*
Where ...	Où ...	*oo*
is the electricity?	est l'électricité?	*ay laylektreeseetay*
are the dustbins?	sont les poubelles?	*sawñ lay poobel*

you may hear ...

La redevance campeur est ...	*la ruhduhvoñs koñpuhr ay*	The camper's fee is ...
Une taxe de séjour de trois euros par nuit/par personne	*ewn tax duh sayjoor duh trwaz uroh par nwee/par person*	Tourist tax of €3 per night/ per person

check out 3

At a campsite you ask about the cost of a pitch.

○ Vous avez un emplacement pour une tente?
vooz avay uñ noñplasmoñ poor ewn toñt

- Oui. Pour combien de nuits?
wee poor kawñbyan duh nwee

○ Quatre nuits. C'est combien?
katr nwee. say kawñbyañ

- Alors, emplacement: onze euros, redevance campeur: six euros, taxe de séjour: un euro par nuit.
alor oñplasmoñ awñz uroh ruhduhvoñs koñpuhr seez uroh tax duh sayjoor uñ nuroh par nwee

Q Do you want a pitch for a caravan or a tent?
How much is it altogether?

self-catering & youth hostels

I'd like to rent ...	Je voudrais louer ...	*juh voodray looay*
the flat.	l'appartement.	*lapartuhmoñ*
the house.	la maison.	*la mayzawñ*
When are the dustbins emptied?	Quand est-ce qu'on ramasse les ordures?	*koñteskawñ ramas layz ordewr*
Do we have to sort the waste? (for recycling)	Est-ce qu'il faut trier les déchets?	*eskeel foh treeay lay dayshay*
Are there any additional costs?	Il y a des charges en supplément?	*eelya day sharj oñ sewplaymoñ*
Can I hire ...	Je peux louer ...	*juh puh looay*
a sleeping bag?	un sac de couchage?	*uñ sak duh kooshaj*
some sheets?	des draps?	*day dra*
Do you have a cot?	Vous avez un lit d'enfant?	*vooz avay uñ lee doñfoñ*
What time do you lock up?	Vous fermez à quelle heure?	*voo fermay a kel uhr*
Is the flat/ gîte/hostel suitable for a wheelchair?	L'appartement/ Le gîte/L'auberge est adapté(e) aux fauteuils roulants?	*lapartuhmoñ/ luh jeet/lohberj ayt adaptay oh fohtuhy rooloñ*
Is there internet access (near) here?	On peut se connecter à l'internet (près d')ici?	*awñ puh suh konektay a lañternet (pre d)eesee*
How does the ... work?	Comment marche ...	*komoñ marsh*
heating	le chauffage?	*luh shohfaj*
boiler	la chaudière?	*la shodyer*

Somewhere to Stay

you may hear ...

Ça marche comme ça.	*sa marsh kom sa*	It works like this.
Il y a un compteur pour l'électricité.	*eelya uñ kawñtuhr poor laylektreeseetay*	There's a meter for the electricity.
haute saison	*oht sayzawñ*	high season
basse saison	*bas sayzawñ*	low season
Vous pouvez laisser la clé chez le voisin.	*voo poovay laysay la klay shay luh vwazañ*	You can leave the key with the neighbour.

check out 4

You are finding out about renting a house.

○ Je voudrais louer la maison. C'est combien?
juh voodray looay la mayzawñ. say kawñbyañ

- C'est quatre cent cinquante euros par semaine.
say katr soñ sañkoñt uroh par suhmen

○ L'électricité est comprise?
laylektreeseetay ay kawñpreez

- Oui, le chauffage aussi.
wee luh shohfaj ohsee.

○ Je peux voir la maison?
juh puh vwar la mayzawñ

- Oui, suivez-moi!
wee sweevay mwa

(suivez-moi = follow me)

Q How much does the house cost to rent for a week?
Electricity is included: true or false?

sound check

Take care to distinguish between the 'closed e' and 'open e' sounds in French.
The closed e is pronounced like the 'a' in 'gate':

café *kafay*   avez *avay*

The open e sounds like the 'e' in 'get':

cette *set*   chèque *shek*

Remember too that the sounds aren't always written down in the same way. The closed e, for example, may appear as **é**, **er** or **ez**, while the open sound could be represented by **e**, **è** or **ê**.

The sounds **ai** and **aî** can be pronounced as either a 'closed' or 'open' e (although **ail** is pronounced like the i in 'site'):

j'ai *jay*   fraîche *fresh*   lait *leh*

Use the following words to practise:

saison *sayzawñ* voudrais *voodray*   tête *tet*
taille *tiy*   discothèque *deeskohtek*

try it out

match it up

Match the phrases to make complete sentences.

1	Désolé, c'est …	**a**	voir la chambre?
2	Le dîner est servi …	**b**	à grand lit.
3	À quelle heure …	**c**	complet.
4	Une chambre …	**d**	remplir la fiche?
5	Je peux …	**e**	est le petit déjeuner?
6	Pourriez-vous …	**f**	à partir de dix-neuf heures.

Somewhere to Stay

mind the gap

Fill in the blanks to complete the missing words. All the words start with c.

1 No vacancies: c _ _ _ _ _ _

2 Not cheap: c _ _ _

3 How much? c _ _ _ _ _ _

4 A room to sleep in: c _ _ _ _ _ _

5 Bigger than a tent, on wheels: c _ _ _ _ _ _ _ _

6 Regulates the temperature in your room:
c _ _ _ _ _ _ _ _ _ _ _ _

as if you were there

You're in a hotel, asking about a room for two adults. Follow the prompts to play your part.

(Say good afternoon and you'd like a room)
Pour combien de personnes?

(Say for two)
Que voulez-vous comme chambre? Il y a une chambre à deux lits et il y a une chambre à grand lit.

(Say the room with the double bed, please)
Bon, d'accord. Pour combien de nuits?

(Say for three nights and ask how much it is per night)
Cinquante-cinq euros.

(Finally, ask whether breakfast is included)
Le petit déjeuner est en supplément.

linkup

key phrases

Vous avez une chambre à grand lit?	**Do you have** a double room?
Je voudrais une chambre avec salle de bains.	**I'd like** a room with a bathroom.
Il y a un ascenseur?	**Is there** a lift?
Il n'y a pas d'eau chaude.	**There isn't any** hot water.
La télévision **ne marche pas**.	The television **isn't working**.
Le petit déjeuner est **à quelle heure**?	**What time** is breakfast?

describing things

All nouns in French (words for things, people, places or ideas) are either masculine or feminine. You can recognise masculine nouns as they are used with le or un (meaning 'the' or 'a'), while feminine words use la or une.

For more on gender see the Language Builder, p131.

The ending of the adjective, or describing word, changes depending on the gender (masculine/feminine) and number (singular/plural) of the word it refers to:

Il y a un **petit** restaurant. There is a small restaurant.
La chambre est **petite**. The room is small.
un **grand** lit a double bed (literally, a big bed)
une **grande** piscine a big swimming pool

Notice the extra 'e' on the adjective when it refers to a feminine word.

Adding an 'e' is a common way to change masculine adjectives to feminine. It often affects how you pronounce the word, as the final consonant is sounded. For example: petit *puhtee* becomes petite *puhteet*, grand *groñ* changes to grande *groñd*.

Adjectives have plural endings too:
Les lits sont **petits**. (mpl) The beds are small.
Les chambres sont **petites**. (fpl) The rooms are small.

word order

When you say 'The hotel is very expensive' in French, the word order is the same as in English: L'hôtel est très cher.
But if you say 'an expensive hotel', the word order is different: un hôtel cher. Adjectives in French generally come after the word they describe:
une lampe **cassée** a broken lamp
une douche **froide** a cold shower
But some common adjectives come before the noun:
le **premier** étage the first floor
un **grand** gîte a large gite
See a list of other adjectives that come before the noun in the Language Builder, p134.

negatives

To make a sentence negative put **ne** and **pas** around the verb:
La climatisation **ne** marche **pas**. The air conditioning isn't working.
Ce **n**'est **pas** assez cuit. It's not cooked enough.

Always use **de** or **d'** (not **du**, **de la**, **de l'** or **des**) after a negative word:
Nous **n**'avons **pas de** chambres. We haven't got any rooms.
For more on negatives, see the Language Builder, p133.

Buying **Things**

opening hours

Shops Many local shops close on Mondays, and from noon to 2pm every day, but stay open until 8pm. Bakeries often open on Sunday mornings, though you won't be able to shop anywhere else. Some shops (especially in Paris) shut down during August. On holidays, Sunday hours apply.

Banks In larger towns and cities banks tend to remain open all day, but branches in the suburbs and the countryside are likely to close at lunchtimes and on Mondays.

at the tabac

Buy your stamps, newspapers, cigarettes and phone cards at a **tabac** (newsagent's). Note that smoking is now banned in most public places in France.

local crafts

Ceramics Look out for porcelain in Limoges, rustic and North African pottery in the south (especially summer pottery markets – **foires des potiers**), as well as wood-fired terracotta pots and roof tiles. Faïence is made at Moustiers in Provence, and, with distinctive naïve motifs, in Quimper, Brittany. Alsace has attractive cookware – look for kugelhopf cake moulds.

Glass Centres include Biot, north of Cannes – beautiful but pricey 'bubbled' glassware – and Couloubrines (Montpellier region). For crystal go to the Vosges, Arques (Calais region), La Rochère (Hautes-Alpes, France's oldest glassworks), and Passavant-la-Rochère (Saône valley).

Natural soaps and perfumes Provence is the main centre for these; Marseille is famous for its olive oil soaps, and there are several perfumeries in Grasse.

Carving You'll find olive-wood items in Provence. Basque craftsmen carve ornamental canes (makila), wooden toys are made in the Jura region, and wood-carving and furniture-making thrive in the pine-rich Alps and Queyras region.

local delicacies

Each town and village in France boasts its own gastronomic speciality, reflecting the traditions and climate of the area. Try the local **traiteur** (delicatessen) or a good supermarket (sections marked **produits régionaux**). Markets can also be a great place to sample regional products, but remember they usually finish promptly at lunchtime. Larger, nationwide delicatessens include La Comtesse du Barry and Fauchon, specialising in gift foods which are easy to take home. Among these: jars of confits, cassoulet, choucroute, foie gras, goat's cheese, peat-smoked garlic, Provençal lavender honey, local jams and sauces, cold-pressed olive oil from the south, as well as strings of garlic, dried sausage, sea-salted butter from Brittany, Normandy cider and calvados.

cheeses

You'll find most of the following all over France, but look out for local specialities as well:

Paris and the Loire Brie, made in Melun, Meaux, Nangis and Montereau; Crottin de Chavignol, Selles-sur-Cher (charcoal-dusted soft goat's cheese).

The Alps Morbier (in the Jura), Gruyère, Emmenthal, Vacherin, Reblochon, Tomme de Savoie, St-Marcellin – mostly hard cheeses.

The Massif Central Cantal, Salers, Saint-Nectaire, Fourme d'Ambert, Bleu d'Auvergne, Roquefort (blue, made with ewe's milk).

Normandy Camembert, Pont-l'Évêque, Livarot.

The North Maroilles.

▰ sweets

There are many delicious treats to try. **Les bêtises de Cambrai** are coffee-caramel sweets from the Calais region. In Languedoc look for **Berlingots de Pézenas**, handmade, naturally-flavoured boiled sweets. **Calissons** (iced honey and almond sweetmeats) are popular in Aix-en-Provence, as are **Canelés**, batter cakes caramelised in tiny copper moulds, in the Bordeaux region. In Provence try **marrons glacés** (preserved sweet chestnuts), and in Toulouse, **violettes** (crystallised violets) are a local favourite.

▰ wine

Stock up on AOC or good-quality **vin de pays** at the local **cave**

coopérative (collective), in **bidons** (plastic containers) or bottles. Visitors to major wine-producing regions (Bordeaux, Bourgogne) can follow signs for **dégustation** (tasting), but should also arm themselves with a guidebook rating particular châteaux or domaines, best years, etc. Here's a brief guide to 'label language'.

Appellation d'Origine Contrôlée The AOC is a guarantee of quality and denotes wines from a clearly-defined area, made to certain specifications. The year of production is always indicated. Additional distinctions include Grand Vin de Bordeaux, Grand Vin de Bourgogne, etc.

Vin de pays Non-AOC regional wine – often perfectly drinkable.

Vin de table Basic plonk.

Mis en bouteille au château (or **à la propriété**) The wine is produced and bottled at a particular vineyard. Without this, labels referring to one property (or **domaine**) may simply indicate the grower of the grapes: the wine itself may be made or bottled elsewhere.

A private **négociant** (dealer) or **cave coopérative** may buy in grapes from various growers – often perfectly good AOC, and cheaper.

phrasemaker

phrases to use anywhere

you may say ...

Do you have	Avez-vous/	*avay voo/*
any ...	Vous avez ...	*vooz avay*
bread?	du pain?	*dew pañ*
stamps?	des timbres?	*day tañbr*
How much is that?	Ça fait combien?	*sa fay kawñbyañ*
I'd like ...	Je voudrais ...	*juh voodray ...*
please.	s'il vous plaît.	*seelvooplay*
some ham	du jambon	*dew joñbawñ*
some eggs	des œufs	*dayz uh*
some cheese	du fromage	*dew fromaj*
a bit more/less	mettez plus/moins	*metay plews/mwañ*
I'd like another.	J'en voudrais	*joñ voodray*
	un autre/une autre.	*uñ nohtr/ewn ohtr*
May I try some?	Je peux goûter?	*juh puh gootay*
What is it?	Qu'est-ce que c'est?	*keskuhsay*
this one	celui-ci/celle-ci	*suhlwee-see/sel-see*
that one	celui-là/celle-là	*suhlwee-la/sel-la*
That's all.	C'est tout.	*say too*
It's too expensive.	C'est trop cher.	*say tro sher*
Can I pay by	Je peux payer avec	*juh puh payyay avek*
credit card?	une carte de crédit?	*ewn kart duh kraydee*
Can I have a bag?	Je peux avoir un sac?	*juh puh avwar uñ sak*

you may hear ...

Je peux vous aider?	*juh puh vooz ayday*	Can I help you?
Désolé(e).	*dayzohlay*	Sorry.
Voilà.	*vwala*	Here you are.
Combien en voulez-vous?	*kawñbyañ oñ voolay voo*	How much/many do you want?
Il n'en reste plus.	*eel noñ rest plew*	It's sold out.
Autre chose?	*ohtr shohz*	Anything else?
C'est tout?	*say too*	Is that all?
Ça fait ... euros (en tout).	*sa fay ... uroh (oñ too)*	That's ... euros (altogether).
Tapez votre code secret.	*tapay votr kod suhkray*	Type your PIN.
C'est pour offrir?	*say poor ofreer*	Is it a present?
Vous voulez un paquet-cadeau?	*voo voolay uñ pakay kadoh*	Would you like it gift-wrapped?

shops

butcher's	la boucherie	*la booshree*
bakery	la boulangerie	*la booloñjree*
bookshop and stationer's	la librairie-papeterie	*la leebrayree papetree*
cake shop	la pâtisserie	*la pateesree*
chemist's	la pharmacie	*la farmasee*
covered market	les halles	*lay al*
delicatessen	la charcuterie/ le traiteur	*la sharkewtree/ luh traytuhr*
department store	le grand magasin	*luh groñ magazañ*
(flea) market	le marché (aux puces)	*luh marshay (oh pews)*
general food store	l'alimentation générale (m)	*laleemoñtasyawñ jaynayral*
grocer's	l'épicerie (m)	*laypeesree*

jeweller's	la bijouterie	*la beejootree*
newsagent's	le tabac/le marchand de journaux	*luh taba/luh marshoñ duh joornoh*
off-licence	le débit de vins et spiritueux	*luh daybee duh vañ ay speereetewuh*
post office	la poste	*la post*
shopping centre	le centre commercial	*luh soñtr komersyal*
studio/workshop	l'atelier (m)	*lauhlyay*
travel agent's	l'agence de voyage (f)	*lajoñs duh vwayaj*

quantities

(half) a kilo	un (demi-)kilo	*uñ (duhmee) keeloh*
100 grammes	cent grammes	*soñ gram*
another	un/une autre	*uñ nohtr/ewn ohtr*
(half) a litre	un (demi-) litre	*uñ (duhmee) leetr*
a third/a quarter	un tiers/un quart	*uñ tyer/uñ kar*
a little bit	un petit peu	*uñ puhtee puh*
a bag of flour	un sac de farine	*uñ sak duh fareen*
a bottle of washing up liquid	une bouteille de liquide pour la vaisselle	*ewn bootayy duh leekeed poor la vaysel*

a carton of ...
  milk
  fruit juice
	un carton de ...
	  lait
	  jus de fruits
		*uñ kartawñ duh
		  lay
		  jew duh frwee*

a jar of jam	un pot de confiture	*uñ poh duh kawñfeetewr*
a piece of cake	un morceau de gâteau	*uñ morsoh duh gatoh*
a packet of butter	une plaquette de beurre	*ewn plaket duh buhr*
a slice of ham	une tranche de jambon	*ewn troñsh duh joñbawñ*
a tin/can of tuna	une boîte de thon	*ewn bwat duh tawñ*

a packet of ...
  sweets
  washing powder
	un paquet de ...
	  bonbons
	  lessive
		*uñ pakay duh
		  bawñbawñ
		  leseev*

check out 1

You're at the delicatessen buying some ingredients for a picnic.

○ Bonjour, je peux vous aider?
  bawñjoor juh puh vooz ayday

- Le Roquefort, c'est combien?
  luh rokfor say kawñbyañ

○ Vingt-deux euros le kilo.
  vañtduhz uroh luh keeloh

- Deux cents grammes, s'il vous plaît.
  duh soñ gram seelvooplay

○ Voilà. Autre chose?
  vwala. ohtr shohz

- Quatre tranches de saucisson à l'ail, six tranches de jambon et une plaquette de beurre.
  katr troñsh duh sohseesawñ a liy see troñsh duh joñbawñ ay ewn plaket duh buhr

Q Roquefort costs how much a kilo?
Do you buy six packets or six slices of ham?

fruit & vegetables

apples	les pommes (f)	*lay pom*
apricots	les abricots (m)	*layz abreekoh*
avocado	l'avocat (m)	*lavohka*
bananas	les bananes (f)	*lay banan*
blackberries	les mûres (f)	*lay mewr*
blueberries	les myrtilles (f)	*lay meertee*
cabbage	le chou	*luh shoo*
cauliflower	le chou-fleur	*luh shoofluhr*
cherries	les cerises (f)	*lay suhreez*
figs	les figues (f)	*lay feeg*
French beans	les haricots verts (m)	*layz areekoh ver*
grapefruit	le pamplemousse	*luh ponpluhmoos*
grapes	les raisins (m)	*lay rayzañ*
leeks	les poireaux (m)	*lay pwaroh*
lemons	les citrons (m)	*lay seetrawñ*
lettuce	la laitue	*la laytew*
melon	le melon	*luh melawñ*
mushrooms	les champignons (m)	*lay shoñpeenyawñ*
onions	les oignon (m)	*layz onyawñ*
oranges	les oranges (f)	*layz oroñj*
peaches	les pêches (f)	*lay pesh*
pears	les poires (f)	*lay pwar*
(red/green) peppers	les poivrons (rouges/verts) (m)	*lay pwavrawñ (rooj/ver)*
pineapple	l'ananas (m)	*lananas*
potatoes	les pommes de terre (f)	*lay pom duh ter*
plums	les prunes (f)	*lay prewn*
prunes	les pruneaux (m)	*lay prewnoh*
radishes	les radis (m)	*lay radee*
raisins	les raisins secs (m)	*lay rayzañ sek*
raspberries	les framboises (f)	*lay froñbwaz*
strawberries	les fraises (f)	*lay frez*
tomatoes	les tomates (f)	*lay tomat*
watermelon	la pastèque	*la pastek*

check out 2

You now need some fruit to complete your feast.

- ○ Bonjour, Mademoiselle, avez-vous des cerises?
  bawñjoor madmwazel avay voo day suhreez

- - Désolée, il n'en reste plus ... des fraises?
  daysohlay eel noñ rest plew ... day frez

- ○ C'est combien, les fraises?
  say kawñbyañ lay frez

- - Sept euros cinquante le kilo.
  set uroh sañkoñt luh keeloh

- ○ Un demi-kilo, s'il vous plaît.
  uñ duhmee keeloh seelvooplay

- - Voilà les fraises. Autre chose?
  vwala lay frez. ohtr shohz

- ○ Six bananes ... C'est tout. Ça fait combien?
  see banan ... say too. sa fay kawñbyañ

Q Why are there no cherries?
What's offered instead?

PAUL

La FLUTE

fish & meat

beef	le bœuf	*luh buhf*
chicken	le poulet	*luh poolay*
cod	le cabillaud	*luh kabeeyoh*
fish	le poisson	*luh pwasawñ*
ham	le jambon	*luh joñbawñ*
lamb	l'agneau (m)	*lanyoh*
salmon	le saumon	*luh sohmawñ*
tuna	le thon	*luh tawñ*

bread

you may say ...

Can I have half (of it)?	Vous pouvez m'en donner la moitié?	*voo poovay moñ donay la mwatyay*
Could you slice it?	Vous pouvez le trancher?	*voo poovay luh troñshay*
I'd like ...	Je voudrais ...	*juh voodray*
farmhouse bread.	un pain de campagne.	*uñ pañ duh koñpany*
a large baguette.	un pain restaurant.	*uñ pañ restohroñ*
a long baguette.	une baguette.	*ewn baget*
a narrow baguette.	une ficelle/ une flûte.	*ewn feesell/ ewn flewt*
rye bread.	un pain de seigle.	*uñ pañ duh segl*
sandwich bread.	un pain de mie.	*uñ pañ duh mee*
wholemeal bread.	un pain complet/ bis.	*uñ pañ kawñple/ bees*

(For cakes and pastries, see Menu Reader, p100.)

clothes & accessories

belt	la ceinture	*la sañtewr*
blouse	le chemisier	*luh shuhmeezyay*
coat	le manteau	*luh moñtoh*
dress	la robe	*la rob*
gloves	les gants	*lay goñ*
jumper	le pull	*luh pewl*
long-/short-sleeved	à manches longues/courtes	*a moñsh lawñg/koort*
scarf	le foulard	*luh foolar*
shirt	la chemise	*la shuhmeez*
shoes	les chaussures	*lay shohsewr*
skirt	la jupe	*la jewp*
swimming costume	le maillot (de bain)	*luh miyoh (duh bañ)*
tie	la cravate	*la kravat*
trousers	le pantalon	*luh poñtalawñ*

clothes shopping

you may say ...

I'm just looking, thanks.	Je regarde seulement, merci.	*juh ruhgard suhlmoñ mersee*
I'd like ...	Je voudrais ...	*juh voodray*
a skirt.	une jupe.	*ewn jewp*
a pair of trousers.	un pantalon.	*uñ poñtalawñ*
in ...	en ...	*oñ*
wool/cotton	laine/coton	*len/kotawñ*
silk/leather	soie/cuir	*swa/kweer*
I'm a size 40.	Je fais du quarante.	*juh fay dew karoñt*
Can I try it on?	Je peux l'essayer?	*juh puh lesayyay*
It's too ...	C'est trop ...	*say troh*
tight.	serré.	*seray*
large.	grand.	*groñ*
Do you have anything ...	Vous en avez un(e) ...	*vooz oñ navay uñ/ewn*
smaller?	plus petit(e)?	*plew puhtee(t)*
bigger?	plus grand(e)?	*plew groñ(d)*

Do you have the same in yellow?	Est-ce que vous avez le même en jaune?	*eskuh vooz avay luh mem oñ john*
I like it.	Ça me plaît.	*sa muh play*
I don't like it.	Ça ne me plaît pas.	*sa nuh muh play pa*
It fits.	Ça me va.	*sa muh va*
It doesn't fit.	Ça ne me va pas.	*sa nuh muh va pa*
I'll take it.	Je le/la prends.	*juh luh/la proñ*
I'll think about it.	Je vais réfléchir.	*juh vay rayflaysheer*

you may hear ...

Quelle taille?	*kel tiy*	What size?
Quelle pointure?	*kel pwañtewr*	What shoe size?
Quelle couleur?	*kel kooluhr*	What colour?
Ça vous plaît?	*sa voo play*	Do you like it?

at the department store

you may say ...

Where's the toy department?	Où est le rayon de jouets?	*oo ay luh rayawñ duh jooay?*
Where can I find perfume?	Où sont les parfums?	*oo sawñ lay parfañ*

Is there ...
  an escalator?
  a lift?
	Il y a ...
	  un escalier roulant?
	  un ascenseur?
		eelya
		  uñ neskalyay rooloñ
		  uñ nasoñsuhr

Where are the checkouts?	Où est la caisse?	*oo ay la kes*

you may hear ...

au sous-sol	*oh soo sol*	in the basement
au rez-de-chaussée	*oh ray duh shohsay*	on the ground floor
au premier/ deuxième étage	*oh pruhmyay/ duhzyem aytaj*	on the first/ second floor
maroquinerie	*marokeenree*	leather goods
parfums	*parfañ*	perfumes
produits de beauté	*prodwee duh bohtay*	beauty products
vêtements enfants/ femmes/hommes	*vetmoñ oñfoñ/ fam/om*	children's/women's/ men's clothes

check out 3

You're in a department store, shopping for trousers.

○ Je peux essayer ce pantalon?
   juh puh esayyay suh poñtalawñ

- Oui.
   wee

○ Taille quarante-quatre, c'est trop grand. Vous en avez
  un plus petit?
   tiy karoñt katr say troh groñ. vooz oñ navay uñ plew puhtee

- Voilà. Quarante-deux.
   vwala. karoñt duh

○ ... Ah bon! Ça me va. Avez-vous le même en bleu
  ou en vert?
   ... ah bawñ sa muh va. avay voo luh mem oñ bluh oo oñ ver

- Oui, le voilà en bleu.
   wee luh vwala oñ bluh

○ Bon, ça me plaît. Je le prends. Je peux payer avec une
  carte de crédit?
   *bawñ sa muh play. juh luh proñ. juh puh payyay avek ewn
   kart duh kraydee*

Q What size is the pair of trousers the assistant brings?
    How do you pay?

buying stamps & newspapers

you may say ...

How much is a stamp for the UK?	Un timbre pour le Royaume-Uni, c'est combien?	*uñ tañbr poor luh rwiyom ewnee say kawñbyañ*
for a letter/a postcard	pour une lettre/une carte postale	*poor ewn letr/ewn kart postal*
I'd like to send this to Australia.	Je voudrais envoyer ça en Australie.	*juh voodray oñvwiyay sa oñ nostralee*
Do you have any English newspapers?	Vous avez des journaux anglais?	*vooz avay day joornoh oñglay*
I'd like a phone card.	Je voudrais une télécarte.	*juh voodray ewn taylaykart*

photography

you may say ...

35mm film	une pellicule de trente-cinq millimètres	*ewn payleekewl duh troñtsañk meeleemetr*
disposable camera	un appareil jetable	*uñ naparayy juhtabl*
Can you develop this?	Pouvez-vous développer ça?	*poovay voo dayvuhlopay sa*
Can you print from this memory card?	Est-ce que vous pouvez imprimer à partir de cette carte mémoire?	*eskuh voo poovay añpreemay a parteer duh set kart maymwar*
When will it be ready?	Ça sera prêt quand?	*sa suhra pre koñ*

you may hear ...

aujourd'hui/demain	*ohjoordwee/duhmañ*	today/tomorrow
dans une heure/trois jours	*doñ(z) ewn uhr/trwa joor*	in one hour/three days
Vous voulez des doubles?	*voo voolay day doobl*	Do you want duplicate copies?
Mat ou brillant?	*ma oo breeyoñ*	Matt or gloss (finish)?
En quel format?	*oñ kel forma*	What size?

check out 4

You're trying to find your way around a large French department store.

 Excusez-moi, Monsieur, où est le rayon des sports?
exkewzay mwa muhsyuh oo ay luh rayawñ day spor

- Au deuxième étage, Madame.
  oh duhzyem aytaj madam

○ Merci. Il y a un ascenseur?
  mersee. eelya uñ nasoñsuhr

- Oui, bien sûr. Il est là-bas, à côté des jouets.
  wee byañ sewr. eel ay la ba a kohtay day jooay

  (là-bas = over there)

Q Is the sports department on the second or third floor?
Where is the lift?

sound check

The **r** sound in French is scraped in the back of the throat, which doesn't always come naturally for English speakers! Try to make the back of your tongue touch the roof of your mouth and breathe.

Practise your **r** by saying these words aloud:

beurre	*buhr*	voudrais	*voodray*
boucherie	*booshree*	rouge	*rooj*
pharmacie	*farmasee*	grammes	*gram*
mandarine	*moñdareen*	crème	*krem*

try it out

question time

Choose the correct answer to these three questions.

1 Vous avez du pain complet?
   a) Ça fait trois euros soixante.
   b) Celui-là? C'est un baba au rhum.
   c) Non, désolé, il n'en reste plus.

2 Est-ce que la chemise verte vous plaît?
   a) Oui, c'est trop serré.
   b) Non, je pense que je préfère la rouge.
   c) Ce pantalon me va.

3 C'est pour offrir?
   a) Oui, c'est un cadeau.
   b) Oui, celle-là me plaît bien.
   c) J'en voudrais un autre, s'il vous plaît.

as if you were there

You're in a cake shop buying some pastries. Follow the prompts to play your part.

Bonjour, je peux vous aider?
(Say hello, and point to a tart and say you'd like that.
Then ask what it is)
C'est une tarte aux pommes.
(Say good and ask for another one. Ask how much it is)

linkup

key phrases

Est-ce que vous avez des timbres?	**Do you have** any stamps?
Donnez-moi deux kilos, s'il vous plaît.	**I'll have [Give me]** two kilos, please.
Je voudrais une tarte aux pommes.	**I'd like** an apple tart.
Où est le rayon de papeterie?	**Where's** the stationery department?
C'est combien, la jupe/ les chaussures?	**How much** is this skirt/ are these shoes?
J'aime ce tee-shirt.	**I like** this T-shirt.
Vous avez un tee-shirt moins cher?	**Do you have** a cheaper T-shirt?

quantity

You'll meet the word **de** a lot when talking about quantities:

beaucoup de fraises a lot of strawberries
un peu de fromage a bit of cheese
Combien de baguettes? How many baguettes?
(un peu) **plus de** pâté (a bit) more pâté
(un peu) **moins de** moutarde (a bit) less mustard

Notice that it's always **de** when you mention a quantity, regardless of the gender and number of the thing you're talking about.

asking about availability

When out shopping, you can use these phrases to ask for what you want:

Vous avez ...? Est-ce que vous avez ...?   Do you have ...?
Il y a ...? Est-ce qu'il y a ...?   Is there/Are there ...?

For example:
Vous avez **de la** lessive?   Do you have any washing powder?
Il y a **du** pain?   Is there any bread?
Est-ce que vous avez **de l'**eau minérale?   Do you have any mineral water?
Vous avez **des** melons?   Do you have any melons?

Notice that the words for 'any' or 'some' have different forms (du, de la, de l' and des), depending on the gender and number of what follows.

This is explained in more detail in the Language Builder, p132. ┄┄┄┄⟩

more & less

To ask for more or less of something, use plus and moins. In English this is often expressed by adding -er to an adjective, e.g. cheaper. These words go before the adjective, regardless of whether the adjective is before or after the noun:

Est-ce que vous avez du parfum **moins cher**?   Do you have any cheaper perfume? (literally, Do you have any perfume less expensive?)
Vous avez une **plus grande** tarte?   Have you got a bigger tart?

Café **Life**

Cafés, brasseries and bars with pavement terraces and infinite opening hours are a part of French daily life. You'll find snacks and light lunches served throughout most of the day; alcohol and soft drinks from 7am to 1am.

Ordering **le petit déjeuner complet** (set breakfast of coffee, juice and pastries) in a local café may be cheaper than eating in your hotel. Fixed-price lunch menus are also good value. Drinks are expensive **à la terrasse** (on the terrace), and cheaper **au comptoir** (at the bar). Measures and prices are shown on the **tarif des consommations** (price list) at the bar. Pay your waiter: he will bring the bill with your order, give change, tear the slip and leave it on the table. Alternatively, leave the right money (plus a small tip), or take the bill to pay at the bar.

what to drink

Some specialities include:
Pastis Aniseed aperitif popular in the south-east, mixed with water.
Kir White wine with fruit liqueur, usually **cassis** (blackcurrant). **Kir royal** is made with champagne.
Eaux de vie Fruit liqueurs (often digestifs). Try kirsch (cherry), genièvres (juniper-based), or one of the Limousin varieties.
Calvados Normandy's cider liqueur is drunk any time with coffee (**un café-calva**).
Chartreuse Green herb liqueur from Voiron, delicious straight, with tonic, or with hot chocolate.
Beers Always **blonde** (i.e. lager) unless **brune** is specified. 'Un seize' is short for 'Kronenbourg 1664'.
Pressés Freshly-squeezed lemon or orange juice on ice, served à **l'eau** (with a jug of water).
Sirops Fruit or mint cordial, served with water, or sometimes as a shot of flavour in beer.

phrasemaker

asking what there is

Do you have any ...	Avez-vous ...	*avay voo*
apple juice?	du jus de pomme?	*dew jew duh pom*
omelettes?	des omelettes?	*dayz omlet*
What do you have to eat/drink?	Qu'est-ce qu'il y a à manger/boire?	*keskeelya a moñjay/bwar*
What kind of ... do you have?	Qu'est-ce que vous avez comme ...	*keskuh vooz avay kom*
sandwiches	sandwichs?	*soñdweetsh*
fruit juice	jus de fruits?	*jew duh frwee*
ice cream	glaces?	*glas*
What's in it?	Qu'est-ce qu'il y a dedans?	*keskeelya duhdoñ*

you may hear ...

Vous désirez?	*voo dayzeeray*	What would you like?
Désolé(e), il n'en reste plus.	*dayzohlay eel noñ rest plew*	I'm sorry, we've run out.
Il y a ...	*eelya*	There is/are ...
du jambon.	*dew joñbawñ*	ham.
des moules.	*day mool*	mussels.
Quel parfum?	*kel parfañ*	Which flavour? (ice cream)
fraise, pistache, chocolat	*frez, peestash, shokohla*	strawberry, pistachio, chocolate

ordering

you may say ...

I'd like ...	Je voudrais ...	*juh voodray*
a cheese sandwich.	un sandwich au fromage.	*uñ soñdweetsh oh fromaj*
a green salad.	une salade verte.	*ewn salad vert*
half a pint.	un demi. (25cl)	*uñ duhmee*
a vanilla ice cream.	une glace à la vanille.	*ewn glas a la vaneey*
Another one.	Un(e) autre.	*uñ nohtr/ewn ohtr*
with/without ...	avec/sans ...	*avek/soñ*
butter	beurre	*buhr*
cream	crème	*krem*
chips	frites	*freet*

you may hear ...

Avec des glaçons/ du citron?	*avek day glasawñ/ dew seetrawñ*	With ice/ lemon?
Lequel?/Laquelle?	*luhkel/lakel*	Which one?
Payez à la caisse.	*payyay a la kes*	Pay at the till.
C'est un self-service.	*sayt uñ self servees*	It's self-service.
Tout de suite!	*too duh sweet*	Right away!

other useful phrases

you may say ...

Where is/are ... please?	Où sont ... s'il vous plaît?	*oo sawñ ... seelvooplay*
the cutlery	les couverts	*lay koover*
the toilets	les toilettes	*lay twalet*
Can I have ...	Je peux avoir ...	*juh puh avwar*
a straw?	une paille?	*ewn piy*
an ashtray?	un cendrier?	*uñ soñdreeay*
Is service included?	Le service est compris?	*luh servees ay kawñpree*
The bill, please.	L'addition, s'il vous plaît.	*ladeesyawñ seelvooplay*

Café **Life**

Service en sus/ à la discrétion de la clientèle.	*servees oñ sews/ a la deeskraysyawñ duh la kleeoñtel*	Service extra/ at the customer's discretion.

alcoholic drinks

aperitif	un apéritif	*uñ napayreeteef*
... beer	une bière ...	*ewn byer*
draught	à la pression	*a la presyawñ*
bottled	en bouteille	*oñ bootayy*
lager	blonde	*blawñd*
dark	brune	*brewn*
brandy	un cognac	*uñ konyak*
dry/sweet cider	un cidre brut/doux	*uñ seedr brewt/doo*
gin and tonic	un gin-tonic	*uñ jeen toneek*
rum	un rhum	*uñ ruhm*
plum brandy	une mirabelle	*ewn meerabel*
port	un porto	*uñ portoh*
shandy	un panaché	*uñ panashay*
sherry	un xérès	*uñ ksayres*
... wine	vin ...	*vañ*
white/red/rosé	blanc/rouge/rosé	*bloñ/rooj/rohzay*
dry/sweet	sec/doux	*sek/doo*
sparkling/fortified	mousseux/cuit	*moosuh/kwee*
table	de table/ordinaire	*duh tabl/ordeener*
house	réserve du patron	*rayzerv dew patrawñ*

hot drinks

small black coffee	un café	*uñ kafay*
coffee with cream	un (café) crème	*uñ (kafay) krem*
... coffee	un café ...	*uñ kafay*
milky	au lait	*oh lay*
extra-strong/weak	serré/léger	*seray/layjay*
filtered	filtre	*feeltr*
strong black coffee with splash of milk	une noisette	*ewn nwazet*

an espresso	un express	*uñ nexpres*
decaffeinated coffee	un décaféiné	*uñ daykafayeenay*
tea ...	un thé ...	*uñ tay*
black	nature	*natewr*
with milk	au lait	*oh lay*
with lemon	au citron	*oh seetrawñ*
herbal tea	une infusion/	*ewn añfewzyawñ/*
	une tisane ...	*ewn teezan*
camomile tea	de camomille	*duh kamomeey*
verbena tea	de verveine	*duh verven*
mint tea	un thé à la menthe	*uñ tay a la moñt*
hot chocolate	un chocolat chaud	*uñ shokohla shoh*

soft drinks

soft drinks	boissons sans alcool	*bwasawñ soñz alkol*
fresh lemon	un citron pressé	*uñ seetrawñ presay*
... juice	un jus ...	*uñ jew*
apple	de pomme	*duh pom*
grape	de raisin	*duh rayzañ*
grapefruit	de pamplemousse	*duh poñpluhmoos*
(diet) cola	un coca (sans sucre)	*uñ kohka (soñ sewkr)*
lemonade	une limonade	*ewn leemonad*
fizzy orange	une orangeade	*ewn oroñjad*
fizzy fruit cordial	un diabolo	*uñ deeaboloh*
fizzy/still mineral water	l'eau minérale gazeuse/non gazeuse	*loh meenayral gazuhz/nawñ gazuhz*
alcohol-free beer	une bière sans alcool	*ewn byer soñz alkol*
iced coffee	un café frappé	*uñ kafay frapay*

Café **Life**

check out 1

You're enjoying your drinks and decide to have something to eat.

○ Qu'est-ce qu'il y a à manger?
keskeelya a moñjay

- Des sandwichs, des omelettes …
day soñdweetsh dayz omlet

○ Qu'est-ce que vous avez comme sandwichs?
keskuh vooz avay kom soñdweetsh

- Le sandwich au fromage, le sandwich au jambon et le sandwich au thon.
luh soñdweetsh oh fromaj luh soñdweetsh oh joñbawñ luh soñdweetsh oh tawñ

○ Je voudrais un sandwich au jambon et un sandwich au fromage. Et une bière et un jus de pomme, s'il vous plaît.
juh voodray uñ soñdweetsh oh joñbawñ ay uñ soñdweetsh oh fromaj. ay ewn byer ay uñ jew duh pom seelvooplay

Q What sandwiches are available? (see list of snacks below)
What drinks do you order?

snacks

… sandwich	un sandwich …	*uñ soñdweetsh*
cheese	au fromage	*oh fromaj*
ham	au jambon	*oh joñbawñ*
salad	aux crudités	*oh krewdeetay*
tuna	au thon	*oh tawñ*
tuna and olives salad	une salade niçoise	*ewn salad neeswaz*
toasted ham and cheese sandwich	un croque-monsieur	*uñ krok-muhsyuh*
as above + fried egg	un croque-madame	*uñ krok-madam*

... omelette	une omelette ...	*ewn omlet*
plain	nature	*natewr*
mixed herbs	aux fines herbes	*oh feen zerb*
mussels and chips	un moules-frites	*uñ mool freet*
steak and chips	un steak-frites	*uñ stek freet*
(sweet/savoury) pancake	une crêpe/une galette	*ewn krep/ewn galet*
waffle	une gaufre	*ewn gohfr*

check out 2

At a café with friends, you order drinks for everyone.

○ Bonjour, Messieurs-Dames, vous désirez?
bawñjoor maysyuh-dam voo dayzeeray

- Bonjour, un grand crème, une blonde, un verre de vin et un citron pressé, s'il vous plaît.
bawñjoor, uñ groñ krem ewn blawñd uñ ver duh vañ ay uñ seetrawñ presay seelvooplay

○ Vin blanc, rouge ou rosé?
vañ bloñ rooj oo rohzay

- Vin blanc, s'il vous plaît.
vañ bloñ seelvooplay

○ Bien, tout de suite.
byañ too duh sweet

(The waiter comes back with the drinks)

- Voilà, Messieurs-Dames.
vwala maysyuh dam

○ Merci. Ça fait combien?
mersee sa fay kawñbyañ

Q What four drinks do you order?

Café Life

s added to the end of a noun to make it plural is not pronounced:

une paille *ewn piy*   deux pailles *duh piy*
un sandwich *uñ soñdweetsh* deux sandwichs *duh soñdweetsh*

The same applies to adjectives – you add an **s** when the noun they describe is plural, but it doesn't change the way they're pronounced:

un vin blanc *uñ vañ bloñ*   trois vins blancs *trwa vañ bloñ*

try it out

odd one out

Can you find the odd one out in each of the lists below?

1   une omelette, un croque-madame, un jus de raisin, un moules-frites
2   une blonde, un grand crème, un vin rouge, un pastis
3   une gauffre, une glace à la vanille, une crêpe au chocolat, une salade composée

as if you were there

You're in a café ordering drinks and snacks. Follow the prompts to play your part.

Bonjour, Messieurs-Dames.
(Ask for a freshly-squeezed lemon drink without ice, a tea with milk and a glass of white wine)
Autre chose?
(Ask what sandwiches they have)
Fromage, jambon, thon.
(Ask for a tuna sandwich and some chocolate ice cream)
Bien, tout de suite.

linkup

saying what you want

The easiest way of doing this is simply to state the item you want: Deux cafés, s'il vous plaît. Two coffees, please.
You can also say:

Je voudrais deux cafés. I'd like two coffees.

If you're with a group ordering in turn, you can say:

Pour moi, un panaché. A shandy **for me**.

French uses the verb prendre (to take), where we would say 'have' in English: **Je prends** un croque-monsieur. **I'll have** a toasted ham and cheese sandwich.

flavours & fillings

French uses **à** to talk about food flavours and fillings:

un thé **à la** menthe mint tea

un sandwich **au** fromage a cheese sandwich

une omelette **aux** fines herbes a mixed herb omelette

À can be followed by **la** or **l'**, but if it's followed by a masculine word (**le** fromage) or a plural (**les** fines herbes) it becomes **au** and **aux** respectively.

Eating **Out**

where to eat

Restaurants and bistros open from around 11.30am to 2.30pm and roughly 7.30pm to 10.15pm (though you're never hassled to leave). Some may close on a Sunday or Monday. Book ahead for busy Sunday lunchtimes. Excellent-value set menus are posted outside (**menu à prix fixe** or **menu touristique**), though these may only be available at lunch. If you're in a hurry, look for **formules express** or **repas d'affaires** (business specials), typically two courses and wine. Some restaurants specialise in **poissons** and **fruits de mer** (fish and seafood) or **grillades** (grills), while others have a particular regional focus, and of course there's always classical French, from haute cuisine to hearty bistro fare. Also popular are ex-colonial cuisines, particularly North African and Vietnamese. **Brasseries** are café-style bars, though usually serving more substantial meals. Open from morning till late.

Cafétérias Cheap self-service eateries found in shopping centres and hypermarkets.
Chambres d'hôte and fermes-auberges may serve dinner, often using local produce – highly recommended!
Crêperies (licensed) open from lunchtime till late, serving savoury and sweet pancakes, salads, etc.
Pizzerias For an authentic taste, look for **au feu de bois** (wood-fired oven).
Salons de thé (tea rooms) open from around 9am to 7pm, serving pastries and light lunches.
A ban on smoking in restaurants, cafés, hotels and clubs is due from January 2008, and in other public places from February 2007.

eating requirements

Vegetarians Crêperies, pizzerias and tea rooms have the most options. In restaurants, try **salades composées** (mixed salads) or omelettes, but check for **lardons** (bacon bits).

Children The French attach great importance to introducing young children to the pleasure of good food. There are often smaller portions of the fixed-price menu available. You can ask for baby food to be heated and for **une chaise haute** (a high chair).

Allergies French restaurants tend to be less aware of food allergies than those in the UK. Note for nut allergy sufferers: there is no generic word for 'nuts'. Strictly speaking, **noix** refers only to walnuts, so it's safer to say **fruits à coque**, or **fruits secs** (which means both nuts and dried fruit).

what to try

A full-scale French meal can have six courses: apéritif, entrée, fish, a main course, salad, cheese and dessert. Smart places may serve sorbet and **eau-de-vie** to refresh the palate after the fish. Wines and digestifs are integral to the meal. Service is usually included in the prices. Here are a few of the many regional specialities to look out for:

Bouillabaisse (Marseille) Thick Mediterranean fish and seafood soup, served with toasted bread and **rouille** (pepper paste).

Cassoulet (South-West) Chunky pork sausages, preserved goose or duck (**confit**) and white haricot beans baked in a pot.

Choucroute (Alsace) Preserved cabbage, gammon, smoked bacon joints and sausages baked in white wine with cloves and juniper berries.

Couscous royal Spicy sausage (**merguez**), chicken and lamb in a broth of chickpeas, carrots, tomatoes, served with couscous and fiery harissa sauce.

Plateau de fruits de mer (Brittany) Lobster, langoustines, oysters, mussels, cockles, clams, small crabs and prawns, with rye bread and mayonnaise.

Soupe au pistou (Provence) Three-bean stew with **pistou** (ground pine nuts, parmesan, garlic, olive oil) and **pain de campagne**.

Raclette (Savoy Alps) Potatoes and cold meats covered in melted raclette cheese.

Eating Out

phrasemaker

finding somewhere to eat

Is there a good restaurant nearby?	Il y a un bon restaurant dans le quartier?	*eelya uñ bawñ restohroñ doñ luh kartyay*
I'd like to book a table for ... tomorrow night. tonight at 8pm.	Je voudrais réserver une table pour ... demain soir. ce soir à huit heures.	*juh voodray rayzervay ewn tabl poor* *duhmañ swar* *suh swar a weet uhr*
Do you have a table for two?	Vous avez une table pour deux personnes?	*vooz avay ewn tabl poor duh person*
I have a reservation.	J'ai une réservation.	*jay ewn rayzervasyawñ*
It's in the name of ...	C'est au nom de ...	*sayt oh nawñ duh ...*

you may hear ...

Désolé(e), on n'a plus de place pour ce soir.	*dayzohlay, awñ na plew duh plas poor suh swar*	Sorry, we're full for tonight.
Revenez dans une petite demi-heure.	*ruhvuhnay doñz ewn puhteet duhmee uhr*	Come back in about half an hour.

asking about the menu

you may say ...

The menu, please.	La carte, s'il vous plaît.	*la kart seelvooplay*
Is there a menu of the day?	Il y a un menu du jour?	*eelya uñ muhnew dew joor*
Have you got any ... mussels? artichokes? seafood?	Avez-vous ... des moules? des artichauts? des fruits de mer?	*avay voo* *day mool* *dayz arteeshoh* *day frwee duh mer*
What do you recommend?	Qu'est-ce que vous recommandez?	*keskuh voo ruhkomoñday*

What's the local speciality?	Quelle est la spécialité régionale?	*kel ay la spaysyaleetay rayjyonal*
What's this?	Qu'est-ce que c'est?	*keskuh say*
Is it strong/spicy?	C'est fort/épicé?	*say for/aypeesay*

you may hear ...

Vous désirez?	*voo dayzeeray*	What would you like?
Vous voulez commander?	*voo voolay komoñday*	Are you ready to order?
Aujourd'hui, nous avons ...	*ohjoordwee nooz avawñ*	Today, we have ...
C'est ... un gros poisson. une sorte de champignon.	*say uñ groh pwasawñ ewn sort duh shoñpeenyawñ*	It's ... a large fish. a type of mushroom.
Désolé(e), nous n'avons pas de ...	*dayzohlay noo navawñ pa duh*	Sorry, we haven't got any ...

ordering

you may say ...

I'll have ... that. the 20-euro menu. a green salad.	Je prends ... ça. le menu à vingt euros. une salade verte.	*juh proñ sa luh muhnew a vañt uroh ewn salad vert*
as a ... starter main course side dish	comme ... entrée plat principal plat d'accompagnement	*kom oñtray pla prañseepal pla dakawñpanymoñ*
Does it come with vegetables?	C'est garni?	*say garnee*
Do you do children's portions?	Vous faites des portions-enfants?	*voo fet day porsyawñz oñfoñ*
no dessert/coffee	pas de dessert/café	*pa duh deser/kafay*
rare/medium/ well done	bleu/à point/ bien cuit	*bluh/a pwañ/ byañ kwee*

Eating **Out**

you may hear...

Quelle cuisson?	*kel kweesawñ*	How would you like it cooked?
Vous désirez un dessert?	*voo dayzeeray uñ deser*	Would you like a dessert?
Comme boisson?	*kom bwasawñ*	Anything to drink?

drinks

you may say ...

the drinks list	la carte des boissons	*la kart day bwasawñ*
a (half) bottle/ carafe of wine	une (demi-)bouteille/ carafe de vin	*ewn (duhmee) bootayy/karaf duh vañ*
mineral/tap water	l'eau minérale/ du robinet	*loh meenayral/ dew robeenay*

(For more drinks, see pp77-78.)

on your table

(large) cup	la (grande) tasse	*la (groñd) tas*
fork	la fourchette	*la foorshet*
(small) glass	le (petit) verre	*luh (puhtee) ver*
knife	le couteau	*luh kootoh*
napkin	la serviette	*la servyet*
oil and vinegar cruet	l'huilier (m)	*lweelyay*
salt/pepper	le sel/le poivre	*luh sell/luh pwavr*
plate	l'assiette	*lasyet*
spoon	la cuillère	*la kweeyer*

check out 1

You're in a restaurant, ordering your meal.

○ Bonsoir, Monsieur.
bawñswar muhsyuh

– Il y a un menu du jour?
eelya uñ muhnew dew joor

○ Oui, voilà, Monsieur: un menu à vingt-huit euros
et un menu à dix-neuf euros ...
wee vwala muhsyuh uñ muhnew a vañt weet uroh
ay uñ muhnew a deez nuhf uroh

– Bon. Je prends le menu à dix-neuf euros.
bawñ. juh proñ luh muhnew a deez nuhf uroh

○ Et comme boisson?
ay kom bwasawñ

– Une demi-bouteille de rosé, s'il vous plaît.
ewn duhmee bootayy duh rohzay seelvooplay

Q What price menu do you choose?
What do you order to drink?

eating preferences

you may say ...

I'm allergic ...	Je suis allergique ...	*juh sweez alerjeek*
to nuts.	aux fruits secs.	*oh frwee sek*
to dairy products.	aux produits laitiers.	*oh prodwee laytyay*
Is there ... in it?	Est-ce qu'il y a ... dedans?	*eskeelya ... duhdoñ*
wheat	du blé	*dew blay*
meat	de la viande	*duh la vyoñd*
I'm ...	Je suis ...	*juh swee*
vegetarian.	végétarien(ne).	*vayjaytaryañ/en*
vegan.	végétalien(ne).	*vayjaytalyañ/en*

Eating **Out**

during the meal

you may say ...

Excuse me!	S'il vous plaît!	*seelvooplay*
I've been waiting half an hour!	J'attends depuis une demi-heure!	*jatoñ duhpwee ewn duhmee uhr*
I didn't order this.	Je n'ai pas commandé ça.	*juh nay pa komoñday sa*
Another beer/ bottle of wine.	Une autre bière/ bouteille de vin.	*ewn ohtr byer/ bootayy duh vañ*
More bread, please.	Encore du pain, s'il vous plaît.	*oñkor dew pañ seelvooplay*
It's delicious/ very good.	C'est délicieux/ très bon.	*say dayleesyuh/ tre bawñ*
It's underdone.	Ce n'est pas assez cuit.	*suh nay pa asay kwee*
It's cold/tough.	C'est froid/dur.	*say frwa/dewr*

you may hear ...

Ça se passe bien?	*sa suh pas byañ*	**Everything all right?**
Autre chose?	*ohtr shohz*	**Anything else?**

paying

you may say ...

The bill, please.	L'addition, s'il vous plaît.	*ladeesyawñ seelvooplay*
Do you take credit cards?	Vous acceptez les cartes de crédit?	*vooz akseptay lay kart duh kraydee*
Is service included?	Le service est compris?	*luh servees ay kawñpree*
There's a mistake, I think.	Il y a une erreur, je crois.	*eelya ewn eruhr juh kwa*
We didn't have any beer/any starters.	On n'a pas pris de bière/d'entrées.	*awñ na pa pree duh byer/doñtray*

you may hear ...

Le service est/n'est pas compris.	*luh servees ay/ nay pa kawñpree*	**Service is/isn't included.**

check out 2

Your meal isn't going too smoothly ...

○ Monsieur! S'il vous plaît! J'attends toujours le vin ...
  muhsyuh. seelvooplay. jatoñ toojoor luh vañ

- Oh, excusez-moi, Madame.
  oh exkewzay mwa madam

○ ... et mon steak est très dur.
  ay mawñ stek ay tre dewr

- Je suis vraiment désolé. Je vous en apporte un autre
  tout de suite.
  juh swee vraymoñ dayzohlay. juh vooz oñ naport uñ ohtr too
  duh sweet

○ Et vous pouvez m'apporter un autre couteau aussi,
  s'il vous plaît? Il est sale.
  ay voo poovay maportay uñ nohtr kootoh ohsee
  seelvooplay eelay sal

- Oui, bien sûr.
  wee byañ sewr

  (toujours = still; sale = dirty)

Q There are three problems mentioned. What are they?

Eating **Out**

sound check

ill is usually pronounced as a y sound, like the 'y' in 'yet':

fille *feey*   taille *tiy*

You meet the same sound in other letter combinations:

appareil *aparay*   travail *traviy*

However, there are some exceptions to this rule:

ville *veel*   village *veelaj*

Unfortunately, there's no rule as to whether **il** or **ill** is pronounced as a 'y' or as an 'l' – it's simply a case of listening and learning. Practise on these 'y' sounds:

fauteuil *fohtuhy*   portail *portiy*

détail *daytiy*   maillot de bain *miyoh duh bañ*

try it out

match it up

Which of the responses below best corresponds to each question?

1   Le poulet basquaise, qu'est-ce que c'est?
    a) Ce sont des moules dans une sauce à la crème.
    b) C'est un plat typique de la région, avec des poivrons.
    c) Oui, je vous apporte ça tout de suite.

2   Vous voulez autre chose?
    a) Oui, c'est vraiment très bon.
    b) Non, j'ai commandé le steak-frites.
    c) Oui, deux cafés, s'il vous plaît, et l'addition.

3   Vous pouvez me recommander un bon vin?
    a) Le magret de canard est vraiment excellent.
    b) Oui, bien sûr, et vous voulez des frites avec ça?
    c) Nous avons un bon vin de pays, un rouge.

as if you were there

You're in a Paris restaurant and the waiter comes to take your order. Follow the prompts to play your part.

Vous voulez commander?

(Say you'll have artichokes and the mussels. Order a green salad too)

Très bien. Et comme boisson?

(Ask for a glass of white wine)

linkup

making a request

To ask if you or someone else can do something, say:
Je peux ...? Can I ...?
Vous pouvez...? Pouvez-vous ...? Can you ...?

For example:
Je peux avoir une paille? Can I have a straw?
Vous pouvez répéter, s'il vous plaît? Could you repeat that, please?
Pouvez-vous recommander un bon vin? Can you recommend a good wine?
On peut avoir l'addition? Can we have the bill?

In this last example, **on** means 'we'.
You can read more about on in the Language Builder, p136.········>

talking to you

There are two ways of saying 'you' in French – **vous** and **tu**.
Tu is used to a close friend, a family member or a child:
Tu veux un café? Do you want a coffee?
Qu'est-ce que tu prends? What are you having?

Vous is the polite form of address to strangers, shopkeepers, waiters etc.
Vous avez une carte des boissons? Do you have a drinks list?
Qu'est-ce que vous recommandez? What do you recommend?
With vous, the verb ending is usually **-ez**.

Vous is used to address one person or several people. Tu can only be used to address one person. If you are talking to two close friends or several children, use vous. For more on vous and tu, see the Language Builder, p135.········>

the courses

hors d'œuvres/entrées starters
le plat principal main course
viandes meat dishes
volailles, gibier, venaison fowl, game, venison
plats de poissons, fruits de mer, crustacés fish, seafood, shellfish dishes
légumes vegetables
plateau de fromages selection of cheeses
desserts/entremets desserts
pâtisseries/gâteaux choice of cakes

main cooking styles

à l'ancienne according to a traditional recipe
au bleu cooked in water, white wine and herbs
bouilli boiled
à la broche spit-roasted
en croûte covered with pastry
cru raw
en daube casseroled (with wine)
farci stuffed
flambé brandy poured on food and set alight
fouetté whipped
au four oven-baked
frais/fraîche fresh, chilled
fricassé/au pot stewed
frit fried
fumé smoked
gratiné melted cheese on top
grillé grilled
haché minced
meunière dipped in flour and fried in butter, with lemon juice and parsley
à la normande in a cream-based sauce
poché poached
rôti roast
sauté stir-fried
vapeur steamed

the menu

agneau lamb
aiglefin haddock
ail garlic
amandes almonds
anchois anchovies
andouille(tte) (small) chitterling sausage
anguille eel
artichaut globe artichoke
(pointes d')asperges asparagus (tips)
aubergine aubergine
avocat avocado
baeckeoffe mixed meat and vegetable casserole (Alsace)
bar bass
barquette small boat-shaped pastry/punnet
basilic basil
bâtonnets de crabe crab sticks
bavaroise type of light mousse
bavette à l'échalote beef with shallots
bécasse woodcock
bercy butter, white wine and shallot sauce
betterave beetroot
beurre blanc butter sauce with white wine and vinegar
bifteck beefsteak
  tartare raw steak minced with raw egg, onion and Worcester sauce
bisque rich, shellfish soup
blanquette de veau veal stew in lemon and white sauce
bœuf beef
  à la mode braised beef with red wine and vegetables
  bourguignon cooked in red wine and mushrooms

miroton stewed with onions

ouchée à la reine chicken vol-u-vent

oudin (blanc/noir) (white/lack) pudding (sausage)

ouillabaisse chunky mixed fish oup (Marseille)

ouillon broth

oulettes meatballs

ourride fish stew with garlic nayonnaise

randade de morue salted od creamed with potato

rochet pike

rochette kebab

abillaud cod

abri kid

acahuètes peanuts

aille quail

almar/calamar squid

anard duck

aneton duckling

annelle cinnamon

âpres capers

arbonnade de bœuf beef stewed in beer with onions

arottes carrots

arré d'(agneau) loin of (lamb)

arrelet plaice

assoulet casserole of haricot beans, mutton, pork, goose and sausage (Toulouse)

éleri celery

éleri-rave celeriac

èpes boletus mushrooms

ervelas saveloy (a seasoned, smoked pork sausage)

ervelle brains

hampignons mushrooms
  à la grecque mushrooms in olive oil, herbs and tomato sauce

charcuterie assortment of cooked pork meat, served cold

chateaubriand large fillet steak

chevreuil venison

chips crisps

chou cabbage

chou-fleur cauliflower

chou-navet swede

chou rouge red cabbage

choucroute garnie sauerkraut served with smoked ham, sausages and potatoes

choux de Bruxelles Brussel sprouts

ciboulette chives

civet de (lapin/lièvre) jugged (rabbit/hare) (stewed)

cochon de lait suckling pig

cœurs d'artichauts globe artichoke hearts

colin hake

concombre cucumber

confit d'oie goose preserved in fat

consommé clear soup

contre-filet sirloin

coq au vin chicken in red wine, bacon, onion and mushroom sauce

coquilles St-Jacques scallops served in their shells, in a cream sauce

cornichon gherkin

côte rib

côtelette cutlet/chop

coulis purée-like sauce

crabe crab

crème cream
  dubarry cream of cauliflower soup
  vichyssoise cold cream of leek and potato soup, made with chicken stock

cresson watercress

crevettes grises shrimps

crevettes roses prawns

croque-madame toasted ham and cheese sandwich, with a fried egg

croque-monsieur toasted ham and cheese sandwich
croquettes de poisson fish fingers
croustade pastry shell
crudités assorted raw vegetables with a vinaigrette dressing
cuisses de (grenouille) (frogs') legs
darne thick fish steak
daurade sea bream
dinde/dindon/dindonneau turkey
échalotes shallots
écrevisse crayfish
encornet squid
endive endive/chicory
entrecôte rib steak
épaule de ... shoulder of ...
épinards spinach
escalope escalope (boneless slice of meat)
  de veau milanaise breaded veal escalope with tomato sauce
escargots snails
  à la bourguignonne snails in garlic butter
estragon tarragon
faisan pheasant
faux-filet sirloin
fenouil fennel
fèves broad beans
filet (mignon) (small) fillet
fines herbes mixed herbs
flageolets flageolet beans
flétan halibut
foie liver

de volaille chicken liver
  gras goose or duck liver pâté
fondue bourguignonne meat fondue
frites chips
fromage cheese
  de chèvre goat's cheese
galantine cold poultry or game, i aspic or gelatine
galette savoury (buckwheat) pancake
gamba large prawn (Mediterranean)
garbure thick cabbage soup
germes de soja bean sprouts
gibier game
gigot de ... leg of ...
gingembre ginger
girolle chanterelle mushroom
goujon gudgeon (small freshwater fish)/narrow strips
gras-double tripe
gratin dauphinois sliced potatoes baked in cream
grenouille frog
griotte morello cherry
grive thrush
groseilles blanches whitecurrants
groseilles rouges redcurrants
hachis Parmentier shepherd's pie
hareng herring
haricot de mouton mutton stew with haricot beans
haricots beans
  blancs haricot beans

rouges red kidney beans
verts (French/green) beans
herbes herbs
homard lobster
  à l'américaine lobster in wine,
  tomatoes, shallots and brandy
  thermidor lobster in white
  wine, mushrooms, spices and
  flamed with brandy
huile oil
  d'arachide groundnut oil
  d'olive olive oil
  de tournesol sunflower oil
huîtres oysters
jambon ham
  à l'os ham off the bone
  de Bayonne cured ham
  de Parme Parma ham
jarret knuckle/shin
laitue lettuce
langouste sea crayfish
langue tongue
lapin rabbit
  chasseur rabbit with white
  wine and herbs
lard streaky bacon/fat
lardons diced bacon
lentilles lentils
lièvre hare
limande-sole lemon sole
longe loin
lotte monkfish
loup de mer sea bass
magret de (canard) breast of
(duck)
maïs sweetcorn
maquereau mackerel
marcassin young wild boar
marchand de vin red wine
sauce with shallots
marrons chestnuts
matelote fish stew
  d'anguilles eel stew
médaillons tender loin steaks
menthe mint

merlan whiting
merluche hake
miel honey
mojettes aux jambon haricot
beans, ham and tomatoes
mortadelle Bologna sausage
(a large, spiced, pork sausage)
morue cod
moules mussels
  marinières mussels cooked
  in their shells, in white wine,
  shallots and parsley
moutarde mustard
mouton mutton
mulet grey mullet
nature/au naturel plain
navarin d'agneau lamb stew
with vegetables
navet turnip
noisettes hazelnuts
noisettes d'agneau small
boneless rounds of lamb
noix walnuts
  de cajou cashew nuts
  de coco coconut
  de muscade nutmeg
nouilles noodles
œuf(s) egg(s)
  à la coque soft-boiled egg
  brouillés scrambled eggs
  dur hard-boiled egg
oie goose
oignon onion
olives olives
  farcies stuffed olives
omelette omelette
  norvégienne baked Alaska
  paysanne omelette with
  potatoes and bacon
onglet à l'échalote long, narrow
steak fried with shallots
oseille sorrel
pain bread
  grillé toast
palourdes clams

pan-bagnat moist salad and tuna sandwich in a round loaf (Provence)

pâté pâté
  de campagne coarse pork pâté
  de foie liver pâté

pâtes pasta

pauchoise fish stew (Burgundy)

paupiettes (de veau) rolled and stuffed slices (of veal)

perche perch

perdrix partridge

persil parsley

petite friture whitebait

petits farcis stuffed vegetables

petits pois peas

pieds de porc pig's trotters

pigeon/pigeonneau pigeon

pintade guinea fowl

piperade tomatoes and sweet peppers served with scrambled eggs

pissaladière onion tart with black olives and anchovies

pistache pistachio

plie plaice

poireaux leeks

pois chiches chickpeas

poisson fish
  au court-bouillon fish poached in aromatic stock

poitrine breast

poivre (noir) (black) pepper

poivron jaune/rouge/vert yellow/red/green pepper

pommes de terre potatoes
  allumettes thin fried potatoes
  dauphine croquettes of potato mashed with butter and egg yolks and deep-fried
  duchesse potatoes mashed with butter and egg yolks
  en robe de chambre jacket/baked potatoes
  mousseline creamed potatoes

porc pork

pot-au-feu beef and vegetable stew

potage thick vegetable soup
  bonne femme leek and potato soup
  Crécy carrot soup
  Parmentier potato soup
  printanier mixed vegetable soup

potée hotpot

poule hen, chicken
  au pot chicken poached with vegetables

poulet chicken
  (à la) basquaise chicken Basque-style, in a ham, tomato and pepper sauce
  chasseur chicken in a wine, mushroom and tomato sauce
  marengo chicken with white wine, tomatoes, garlic, mushrooms and shallots

poulpe octopus

poussin spring chicken

purée (de pommes de terre) mashed (potatoes)

quenelle type of meat or fish dumpling/semolina sausage

queue de bœuf oxtail

quiche lorraine bacon, egg and cheese flan

raclette hot melted cheese, eaten with potatoes and pickles

radis radishes

ragoût meat stew/casserole

raie skate

rascasse scorpion fish (used in bouillabaisse)

ratatouille vegetable stew of courgettes, peppers, aubergines, tomatoes and onions

religieuse chocolate or coffee cream puff

rillettes de porc/de saumon potted pork/salmon

ris de veau calf's sweetbreads
riz rice
rognons kidneys
romarin rosemary
rosbif roast beef
romsteck rump (beef)
rouget red mullet
grillé sur feuilles de vigne red
mullet barbecued on vine leaves
(neither gutted nor scaled)
rouille spicy sauce made with
garlic, egg yolk, pepper and oil
saint-pierre John Dory (fish)
(de) saison seasonal/in season
salade salad
  composée/mixte mixed salad
  niçoise tuna, tomato, anchovy
  and olive salad
  russe diced, cooked
  vegetables in mayonnaise
  verte green leaf salad
salmis game stew with wine
and vegetable sauce
salsifis salsify (a root vegetable)
sanglier wild boar
sauce sauce
  aurore white sauce with
  tomato purée
  béarnaise sauce made with
  butter, egg yolks, shallots,
  vinegar and herbs
  béchamel white sauce
  chasseur white wine, shallots,
  tomatoes and mushrooms
  hollandaise egg yolks, butter
  and vinegar sauce
  mornay cheese sauce
  piquante hot, spicy sauce
  provençale tomato, garlic and
  herb sauce
  rémoulade mayonnaise with
  mustard and herbs
saucisse sausage
saucisson salami-style sausage
  sec dried sausage

saumon salmon
sel salt
selle de ... saddle of ...
sole sole
  bonne femme sole in white
  wine and mushrooms
soupe soup
  à l'oignon onion soup, topped
  with cheese and bread
  au pistou thick potato,
  courgette and bean soup
  de pêcheurs Provence-style
  mixed fish soup
spaghettis spaghetti
stea(c)k steak
  haché minced meat
  au poivre steak with
  peppercorns
  tartare raw minced steak
  mixed with raw egg
suprême de (volaille) (chicken)
breast in a cream sauce
tapenade paste made with
olives, anchovies, capers,
mustard, garlic and lemon
tartine slice of bread and butter
terrine pâté
thon tuna
tomates tomatoes
topinambour Jerusalem
artichoke
tournedos thick fillet steak
  rossini thick fillet steak with
  foie gras and truffles, in a
  Madeira sauce
travers spare rib
tripes tripe
  à la mode de Caen tripe
  cooked in cider, Calvados and
  herbs, served with vegetables
truffe/truffé truffle/with truffles
truite trout
turbot turbot
veau calf
velouté creamy soup

venaison venison
viande meat
volaille poultry, chicken
waterzoi de poulet chicken in wine and cream sauce with vegetables

desserts & cakes

beignet doughnut/fritter
charlotte creamy fruit filling in a sponge
chausson aux pommes apple turnover
choux à la crème cream puffs
clafoutis fruit cooked in batter
coupe de fruits fruit salad
coupe glacée ice cream (sundae)
crème cream
  anglaise custard
  brûlée baked cream with burnt sugar topping
  caramel baked custard with caramel sauce
  chantilly whipped cream
crêpe pancake
  suzette pancake with orange sauce, flamed with brandy
fromage blanc soft cream cheese
gaufre waffle/wafer

granité type of sorbet
îles flottantes whisked egg whites floating in custard
kugelhopf rich yeast cake with sultanas (Alsace)
madeleine small sponge cake (often lemon-flavoured)
millefeuilles vanilla cream slice
poire belle Hélène pear with vanilla ice cream and chocolate sauce
profiteroles small choux pastry puffs, filled with cream
sabayon whipped egg yolks with wine and sugar
saint-honoré gâteau of choux pastry puffs and cream
tarte tart
  frangipane almond cream tart
  Tatin apple tart
tartelette small tart
tourteau au fromage cheesecake
yaourt (plain) yoghurt (available as part of the cheese course)

(For a list of fruit see p63.
See Café Life, p74, for speciality drinks.)

Entertainment

what's on

The **Office de Tourisme** can provide details of local events and attractions. Away from tourist centres, look for the smaller **Syndicat d'Initiative**, which may stock free local listings magazines. Online, try **uk.maison-de-la-france.com/infospratiques** for sport and cultural events.

what to see

Music Traditional folk music can be heard at any **bal populaire** (local dance), or the **Fête de la Musique** (free street music nationwide, June 21). Churches regularly host classical concerts (often free); jazz is much-loved, with many festivals: (Cannes – February; Grenoble – March; Vienne and Juan-les-Pins – July).

Theatre and film Local theatres feature programmes of music, dance, cabaret, stand-up comedy and plays. Theatre buffs should head for the Avignon festival in July. Some cinemas show English-language releases in VO (**version originale**), but dubbing (VF or **version française**) is the norm.

Museums Almost every large town has museums of local history, **beaux-arts**, **l'art contemporain**, **les arts décoratifs** (fine, contemporary and decorative art). Museums and galleries usually open on Sundays but close on public holidays and sometimes on Tuesdays.

Football France's cup final is in May. Top league matches involving clubs such as

PSG (Paris-St-Germain) or OM (Olympique de Marseille) are worth a visit.

Traditional sports La joute (boat-jousting) is a great summer spectacle at Lyon and Sète. Also look out for tennis variants: le jeu de paume, la balle au tambourin, la pelote basque.

sports

Canoeing Popular on the gentle, scenic Ardèche, Loire, Tarn and Garonne rivers. Also white-water rafting, especially in the Ardèche and Massif Central.

Diving Try Finistère in Brittany and the crystal-clear waters around the Calanques de Cassis near Marseille.

Windsurfing Head south to the Camargue beaches of Piémanson and Fos, or try the Landes or Brittany (for sailing too).

Cycling Le vélo tout-terrain, VTT (mountain-biking) is very popular. Ask at information offices about organised rides and bike hire.

Golf A licence is compulsory. You can buy one for a modest daily rate. You may have to demonstrate a minimum standard (take your handicap certificate) or pass the carte verte (green card test).

Riding Accompanied treks from gîtes d'étape (see p41) are organised throughout rural France. Provence and the Camargue are popular.

Fishing Fishing tackle shops can supply permits and information. Pyrenean rivers are famous for their trout. Some ports (Brittany, the south-east) operate regular sea-fishing trips.

Winter sports Resorts in the Alps and Pyrenees cater for all winter sports, from downhill and cross-country skiing to snowboarding. French school holidays are very busy.

Pétanque or boules The 'national game', played throughout France on roadsides, beaches, car parks, squares and boulodromes. Players use elaborate techniques to pitch bowls at le cochonnet (piglet).

Walking Extensive network (over 30,000km) of chemins de grande randonnée (GRs: long-distance routes). Local footpaths are well marked. Paths in the south-east may be closed and patrolled in summer owing to forest arson.

Centres de loisirs Activities (often free) on offer in leisure centres include watersports, golf, riding and play areas. Ask at the tourist office.

phrasemaker

getting to know the place

you may say ...

I'd like ...	Je voudrais ...	juh voodray
a town plan.	un plan de la ville.	uñ ploñ duh la veel
an entertainment guide.	un guide des spectacles.	uñ geed day spektakl
Do you have any information in English?	Avez-vous des informations en anglais?	avay voo dayz añformasyawñ oñ noñglay
What is there ... here?	Qu'est-ce qu'il y a ... ici?	keskeelya ... eesee
to see	à voir	a vwar
to do	à faire	a fer
for children	pour les enfants	poor layz oñfoñ
Is there ...	Il y a ...	eelya
a guided tour?	une visite guidée?	ewn veezeet geeday
a bus tour?	un tour en bus?	uñ toor oñ bews
Are there any ...	Il y a ...	eelya
tennis courts?	des courts de tennis?	day koor duh tenees
painting exhibitions?	des expositions de peinture?	dayz expohzeesyawñ duh pañtewr
Can you recommend ...	Vous pouvez me recommander ...	voo poovay muh ruhkomoñday
a museum?	un musée?	uñ mewzay
a good bar?	un bon bar?	uñ bawñ bar
I'm interested in ...	Je m'intéresse ...	juh mañtayres
modern art.	à l'art moderne.	a lar modern

you may hear ...

Qu'est-ce qui vous intéresse?	keskee vooz añtayres	What are you interested in?
Il y a un concert de musique classique.	eelya uñ kawñser duh mewzeek klaseek	There is a classical music concert.

Il y a ...	*eelya*	There are ...
des dégustations de vins.	*day daygewstasyawñ duh vañ*	wine-tasting sessions.
des excursions en bateau.	*dayz exkewrsyawñ oñ batoh*	boat trips.

things to do or see

ballet	un ballet	*uñ balay*
circus	un cirque	*uñ seerk*
film	un film	*uñ feelm*
fireworks	un feu d'artifice	*uñ fuh darteefees*
folk dancing	des danses folkloriques	*day doñs folkloreek*
funfair	une fête foraine	*ewn fet foren*
petanque	la pétanque	*la paytoñk*
play/show	un spectacle	*uñ spektakl*
tennis/rugby/football match	un match de tennis/ rugby/football	*uñ matsh duh tenees/ ruhgbee/footbohl*

places to visit

amusement park	le parc d'attractions	*luh park datraksyawñ*
art gallery	le musée d'art	*luh mewzay dar*
castle/mansion	le château	*luh shatoh*
cathedral	la cathédrale	*la kataydral*
church	l'église (f)	*laygleez*
cinema	le cinéma	*luh seenayma*
(night) club	le club/la boîte de nuit	*luh kluhb/la bwat duh nwee*

golf club/course	le club/terrain de golf	*luh kluhb/terañ duh golf*
ice rink	la patinoire	*la pateenwar*
museum	le musée	*luh mewzay*
(indoor/open air) swimming pool	la piscine (couverte/ en plein air)	*la peeseen (koovert/ oñ plañ ner)*
theatre	le théâtre	*luh tayatr*

getting more information

you may say ...

Where is ...	Où est ...	*oo ay*
the swimming pool?	la piscine?	*la peeseen*
the beach?	la plage?	*la plaj*
the concert hall?	la salle de concert?	*la sal duh kawñser*
Where does the guided tour start?	La visite guidée commence où?	*la veezeet geeday komoñs oo*
What time does it start/finish?	Ça commence/finit à quelle heure?	*sa komoñs/feenee a kel uhr*
When is it open/ closed?	Il est ouvert/ fermé quand?	*eel ay(t) oover/ fermay koñ*
Is it open to the public?	C'est ouvert au public?	*sayt oover oh pewbleek*
Do you need tickets?	On a besoin de billets?	*awñ na buhzwañ duh beeyay*
Where do you buy tickets?	On achète les billets où?	*awñ nashet lay beeyay oo*

you may hear ...

Pas besoin de billets.	*pa buhzwañ duh beeyay*	You don't need tickets.
Désolé(e), il ne reste plus de billets.	*dayzohlay, eel nuh rest plew duh beeyay*	Sorry, it's sold out.
de dix heures trente du matin à sept heures du soir	*duh deez uhr troñt dew matañ a set uhr dew swar*	from 10.30am to 7pm
au guichet	*oh geeshay*	at the ticket office
Ici sur la carte.	*eesee sewr la kart.*	Here on the map.

check out 1

You're in the local tourist office, finding what there is to do and see.

○ Bonjour, Madame, je voudrais un plan de la ville, s'il vous plaît.

bawñjoor madam juh voodray uñ ploñ duh la veel seelvooplay

- Voilà. Qu'est-ce qui vous intéresse?

vwala. keskee vooz añtayres

○ Qu'est-ce qu'il y a à faire et à voir dans la région?

keskeelya a fer ay a vwar doñ la rayjyoñ

- Il y a des excursions en bateau, des musées, un parc d'attractions …

eelya dayz exkewrsyawñ on batoh day mewzay uñ park datraksyawñ

○ Il y a des expositions de peinture?

eelya dayz expohzeesyawñ duh pañtewr

- Oui, au musée d'art.

wee oh mewzay dar

Q What four types of event or activity are mentioned?

getting in
you may say …

Do you have any tickets for …	Avez-vous des billets pour …	*avay voo day beeyay poor*
the Molière play?	la pièce de Molière?	*la pyes duh molyer*
the concert?	le concert?	*luh kawñser*
How much is it?	Ça fait combien?	*sa fay kawñbyañ*
Are there any concessions?	Il y a des réductions?	*eelya day raydewksyawñ*

A family ticket, please.	Un billet familial, s'il vous plaît.	*uñ beeyay fameelyal seelvooplay*
Two tickets, for Saturday night/ tomorrow.	Deux billets, pour samedi soir/ demain.	*duh beeyay poor samdee swar/ duhmañ*
How long does it last?	Ça dure combien de temps?	*sa dewr kawñbyañ duh toñ*
Is the film subtitled?	Le film est sous-titré?	*luh feelm ay soo-teetray*
Is there an interval?	Il y a un entracte?	*eelya uñ noñtrakt*
Is it suitable for children?	Ça convient aux enfants?	*sa kawñvyañ ohz oñfoñ*
Is there wheelchair access?	Il y a un accès pour un fauteuil roulant?	*eelya uñ naxay poor uñ fohtuhy rooloñ*
Is this seat available/taken?	Cette place est libre/occupée?	*set plas ay leebr/okewpay*

you may hear …

Moitié prix pour …	*mwatyay pree poor*	Half price for …
les étudiants.	*layz aytewdyoñ*	students.
les enfants.	*layz oñfoñ*	children.
les personnes âgées.	*lay personz ajay*	senior citizens.
un entracte de vingt minutes	*uñ noñtrakt duh vañ meenewt*	one interval of 20 minutes
en VO/VF (version originale/française)	*oñ vayoh/vayef*	foreign film in original language/dubbed
Il y a des rampes d'accès.	*eelya day roñp daxay*	There are wheelchair ramps.
balcon/loge/ orchestre	*balcon/loj/orkestr*	balcony/box/stalls

swimming & sunbathing

you may say …

Can I use the hotel pool?	Je peux utiliser la piscine de l'hôtel?	*juh puh ewteeleezay la peeseen duh lohtel*
Where are …	Où sont …	*oo sawñ*
the changing rooms?	les vestiaires?	*lay vestyer*
the showers?	les douches?	*lay doosh*

I'd like to hire ...	Je voudrais louer ...	*juh voodray looay*
a parasol.	un parasol.	*uñ parasol*
a sunbed/deckchair.	une chaise longue.	*ewn shayz lawñg*
a windbreak.	un coupe-vent.	*uñ koop-voñ*
a mask and flippers.	un masque et des palmes.	*uñ mask ay day palm*
Can we swim here?	Est-ce qu'on peut nager ici?	*eskawñ puh najay eesee*
Is it safe for children?	Est-ce que c'est sans danger pour les enfants?	*eskuh say soñ doñjay poor layz oñfoñ*

check out 2

You're in an interesting art gallery and hear that there's a guided tour, so try to find out more.

○ Bonjour, Monsieur. La visite guidée commence à quelle heure, s'il vous plaît?

   bawñjoor muhsyuh. la veezeet geeday komoñs a kel uhr seelvooplay

- À neuf heures.

   a nuhf uhr

○ On achète les billets où?

   awñ nashet lay beeyay oo

- Pas besoin de billets!

   pa buhzwañ duh beeyay

○ Ah bon! Où commence la visite?

   ah bawñ. oo komoñs la veezeet

- Ici, Madame.

   eesee madam

 Do you need tickets to go on the tour?

sports

you may say ...

Where can I go ...	Où puis-je ...	*oo pwee juh*
swimming?	nager?	*najay*
fishing?	aller à la pêche?	*alay a la pesh*
Where can we play ...	Où peut-on jouer ...	*oo puht awñ jooay*
tennis?	au tennis?	*oh tenees*
volleyball?	au volley?	*oh volay*
I'd like to take ... lessons.	Je voudrais prendre des cours de ...	*juh voodray proñdr day koor duh*
sailing	voile.	*vwal*
skiing	ski.	*skee*
How much is it per hour/per day?	C'est combien de l'heure/par jour?	*say kawñbyañ duh luhr/par joor*
Where can you go ...	Où peut-on faire ...	*oo puht awñ fer*
cross-country skiing?	du ski de fond?	*dew skee duh fawñ*
ponytrekking/ hiking?	des randonnées équestres/pédestres?	*day roñdonay aykestr/paydestr*
I'd like to hire ...	Je voudrais louer ...	*juh voodray looay*
a tennis racket.	une raquette de tennis.	*ewn raket duh tenees*
a (motor/rowing) boat.	un bateau (à moteur/ à rames).	*uñ batoh (a mohtuhr/ a ram)*
a surf/windsurf board.	une planche de surf/à voile.	*ewn ploñsh duh sewrf/a vwal*
a bike.	un vélo.	*uñ vayloh*

bungee jumping	le saut à l'élastique	*luh soh a laylasteek*
horseriding	l'équitation	*laykeetasyawñ*
ice skating	le patinage sur glace	*luh pateenaj sewr glas*
rock-climbing	la varappe	*la varap*
roller-skating	le patin à roulettes	*luh patañ a roolet*
rollerblading	le patin en ligne	*luh patañ oñ leeny*
sailing	la voile	*la vwal*
scuba diving	la plongée sous-marine	*la plawñjay soo mareen*
skiing	le ski	*luh skee*
snowboarding	le snowboard	*luh snohbord*
surfing	le surf	*luh sewrf*
tennis	le tennis	*luh tenees*
tobogganing	la luge	*la lewj*
waterskiing	le ski nautique	*luh skee nohteek*
windsurfing	la planche à voile	*la ploñsh a vwal*

check out 3

You're interested in trying out one of the activities offered on the beach.

○ Bonjour, je voudrais prendre des cours de ski nautique.
   bawñjoor juh voodray proñdr day koor duh skee nohteek

- Bien sûr, Monsieur!
   byañ sewr muhsyuh

○ C'est combien?
   say kawñbyañ

- C'est trente euros la demi-heure.
   say troñt uhroh la duhmee uhr

Q Do you want to learn windsurfing or waterskiing?
Are the lessons €30 for an hour or for half an hour?

sound check

g is pronounced in three ways, depending on the letter that follows it.

g + **a**, **o**, **u** or a consonant (except **n**) – like 'g' in 'got':

guide *geed*   golf *golf*   programme *prohgram*

g + **n** – like the 'ni' sound in 'onion', shown here as *ny*:

champagne *shoñpany*   Dordogne *dordony*
compagnon *kawñpanyawñ*

g + **e** or **i** – like the s in 'measure', shown as a *j*:

gilet *jeelay*   patinage *pateenaj*
gentil *joñtee*

Use the following words to practise the **g** sound – and look out for more examples in the French around you!

guichet *geeshay*   baguette *baget*   baignoire *baynywar*
lorgnette *lornyet*   plongée *plawñjay*   plage *plaj*

try it out

mind the gap
Use the clues to complete the words for various objects to
do with sports and leisure activities.

1 Je peux les voir à la plage:
des c_ _ _s_ _ l_ _ _ _ _ _

2 Il faut les acheter pour voir un film:
des b_ _ _ _t_

3 On peut en louer une pour jouer au tennis:
une _ _q_ _ _ _e

4 Utile sur un bateau sans moteur:
des r_ _ _ _
(utile = useful)

5 Dans le ciel, la nuit, c'est spectaculaire!
un f_ _ d'_r_ _f_c_
(le ciel = sky)

as if you were there
You're at a museum, asking for an English guidebook.
Follow the prompts to play your part.

Bonjour, vous désirez?
(Say hello and ask for a guidebook to the museum, in English)
Mais oui! Voilà un guide en anglais.
(Say thanks and ask how much it is)
Trois euros, s'il vous plaît.

linkup

J'aime (bien) le ballet.	**I like** ballet **(very much)**.
Est-ce que vous avez un plan de la ville?	**Do you have** a town plan?
Qu'est-ce qu'il y a à voir ici?	**What is there** to see here?
Ça commence **à quelle heure**?	**What time** does it start?
Il y a un terrain de golf?	**Is there** a golf course?
Où peut-on faire des randonnées équestres?	**Where can you** go ponytrekking?
Il est possible de louer des skis?	**Is it possible to** hire skis?

likes, dislikes & preferences

To say what you like, use the verb aimer:
J'aime le théâtre. **I like** the theatre.
Vous aimez l'opéra? **Do you like** opera?
If you really like something:
J'aime bien le golf. **I really like** golf.
J'adore la musique jazz. **I love** jazz music.

To say you don't like something, put **ne** and **pas** around the verb: **Je n'aime pas** la plage. **I don't like** the beach.

To express a preference, use the verb préférer:
J'aime les films anglais, mais je préfère le cinéma français.
I like English films, but I prefer French cinema.
Préféré(e) (literally, preferred) means favourite:
Quel est votre livre préféré? What's your favourite book?

using the infinitive

The infinitive is the part of the verb you'll find in a dictionary:
nager to swim
jouer to play

Infinitives are used in combination with other verbs:
J'adore **danser**. I love dancing. (literally, I love to dance)
Il n'aime pas **regarder** le football. He doesn't like watching football. (literally, he doesn't like to watch football)

The infinitive is also used after the verb aller (to go), to talk about future plans, as we do in English.
Je vais **acheter** les billets. I am going to buy the tickets.
Demain, nous allons **visiter** Aix. Tomorrow, we are going to visit Aix.

Another verb you could use in the same way is vouloir (to want):
Est-ce que tu veux **venir** au cinéma avec moi? Do you want to come to the cinema with me?
Je voudrais **visiter** Paris un jour. I'd like to visit Paris one day.

For more on aller and vouloir, see the Language Builder, p137. ····▶

can & can't

To find out what you can and can't do in a place use
On peut ...? or Peut-on ...? followed by an infinitive. On can translate 'you', 'we' or 'they', depending on context. It can be the equivalent of 'one' in English. See also making a request, p93, and the Language Builder, p136. ····▶

Où peut-on nager? Where can you swim?
On peut faire du ski ici? Can we ski here?
On peut louer des bateaux? Can we hire a boat?

Emergencies

reporting crime

Report all incidents immediately to the **commissariat** (local police), who will provide an insurance report. French police have extensive stop-and-search powers, and may detain anyone for 48 hours with no right to an outside call. If asked to make a **procès-verbal** (statement), take your passport and vehicle registration papers with you. The **gendarmerie nationale** is a military force, dealing with crime outside towns and traffic accidents on motorways.

health

The **service des urgences** (casualty department) of the local hospital should be able to deal with most emergencies. You can also call the **Service d'Aide Médicale d'Urgence**, or SAMU (dial 15), although in rural areas it may be quicker to call the **sapeurs pompiers** (fire service) on 18. Paramedics are known as **secouristes**.

For less urgent cases, **pharmacies** (chemists': with neon green crosses) can give medical advice or recommend a **médecin généraliste** (doctor). (They can also identify any dubious-looking fungi you may pick!) At night, on Sundays or public holidays, call **SOS Médecins** (home visits, usually within the hour); or try the **pharmacie de garde** (duty chemists' – this rotates, look for signs in other chemists' windows).

Consultations must be paid for on the spot in cash or Eurocheques; GPs in private practice – as opposed to those registered with the Department of Health, or **agréé** – charge higher fees. For insurance claims, always ask for the **feuille de soins** form given by the doctor, and make sure it is also stamped by the chemist, with details of any medication bought. EU nationals must have a valid European Health Insurance Card (EHIC) entitling them to free or reduced cost medical care while in France; it is available from UK post offices or online: **www.dh.gov.uk/travellers.**

LA POSTE

Tap water is generally safe to drink – non-drinking water taps are, by law, labelled eau non-potable. Mosquitoes are a nocturnal nuisance everywhere in summer. Meat is served very rare, and sauces (e.g. hollandaise) may contain raw egg. Pregnant women should avoid these and cheeses au lait cru (unpasteurised).

phone calls

If using public phones, you'll need to invest in a télécarte from any tabac or buraliste. Many public phones now take Visa or Mastercard with your PIN.

post offices

La Poste is always signposted, and decked in bright yellow and blue. Opening times vary. Machines relieve the queues in larger offices: weigh your mail, insert cash and take a printed label. You can also buy stamps at tabacs.

car breakdown

Motorways have emergency phones every mile or so; la gendarmerie (motorway police) will locate your call and arrange towing etc. On other roads, call directory enquiries for the numbers of local services (dépannages et remorquages d'automobiles). You'll need to pay on the spot.

travellers with disabilities

Look for the blue and yellow help-point symbol. Public transport is not always geared to less able travellers, although concessions may be offered (e.g. on the Eurostar) – check with the operator. For parking, the international blue scheme applies and there is strict enforcement of the law on disabled parking spaces. For accommodation, check in advance that hotels can meet requirements. Visitors to Paris can hire wheelchairs from the CRF (01 43 73 98 98). For more advice go to: **www.mobile-en-ville.asso.fr www.tourisme-handicaps.org**

useful numbers

Emergencies 112
Ambulance (SAMU) 15
Police and gendarmerie 17
Fire (les pompiers) 18
Directory enquiries 118 218

phrasemaker

emergency phrases

you may say ...

Help!	Au secours!	*oh suhkoor*
Can you help me?	Pouvez-vous m'aider?	*poovay voo mayday*
Does anyone speak English?	Quelqu'un parle anglais?	*kelkuñ parl oñglay*
There's been an accident.	Il y a eu un accident.	*eelya ew uñ naxeedoñ*
A doctor is needed.	Il faut un docteur.	*eel foh uñ doktuhr*
It's urgent!	C'est urgent!	*say ewrjoñ*
Don't move me/him/her!	Ne me/le/la bougez pas!	*nuh muh/luh/la boojay pa*
Where's ... the police station? the hospital?	Où est ... le poste de police? l'hôpital?	*oo ay luh post duh polees lopeetal*
I need an ambulance.	J'ai besoin d'une ambulance.	*jay buhzwañ dewn oñbewloñs*
Where's the nearest ... petrol station? chemist? public phone?	Où est ... le/la plus proche? la station-service la pharmacie la cabine téléphonique	*oo ay ... luh/la plew prosh la stasyawñ servees la farmasee la kabeen taylayfoneek*
thank you	merci	*mersee*
Leave me alone.	Laissez-moi tranquille.	*laysay mwa troñkeel*
I'll call the police.	Je vais appeler la police.	*juh vay aplay la polees*

telling the doctor or dentist

you may say ...

I'd like an appointment with ... a doctor. a dentist.	Je voudrais un rendez-vous avec ... un docteur. un dentiste.	*juh voodray uñ roñdayvoo avek uñ doktuhr uñ doñteest*

I've got ...	J'ai ...	*jay ...*
a cold.	un rhume.	*uñ rewm*
flu.	la grippe.	*la greep*
a rash.	des rougeurs.	*day roojuhr*
shivers.	des frissons.	*day freesawñ*
heartburn.	des brûlures d'estomac.	*day brewlewr destoma*
diarrhoea.	la diarrhée.	*la deeaaray*
I'm coughing a lot.	Je tousse beaucoup.	*juh toos bohkoo*
I'm constipated.	Je suis constipé(e).	*juh swee kawñsteepay*
I've/He's ...	J'ai/Il a ...	*jay/eel a*
been sick all night.	vomi toute la nuit.	*vomee toot la nwee*
It hurts here.	Ça fait mal ici.	*sa fay mal eesee*
I've got ...	J'ai mal ...	*jay mal*
backache.	au dos.	*oh doh*
toothache.	aux dents.	*oh doñ*
a stomach ache.	à l'estomac.	*a lestoma*
earache.	à l'oreille.	*a lorey*
My child has a temperature.	Mon enfant a de la température/fièvre.	*mawñ noñfoñ a duh la toñpayratewr/fyayvr*
She/He feels ...	Elle/Il a ...	*el/eel a*
sick.	la nausée.	*la nohzay*
dizzy.	le vertige.	*luh verteej*
I'm allergic ...	Je suis allergique ...	*juh swee alerjeek*
to antibiotics.	aux antibiotiques.	*ohz oñteebyoteek*
to animals.	aux animaux.	*ohz aneemoh*
to aspirin.	à l'aspirine.	*a laspeereen*
I'm ...	Je suis ...	*juh swee*
diabetic.	diabétique.	*dyabayteek*
pregnant.	enceinte.	*oñsañt*
epileptic.	épileptique.	*aypeelepteek*
HIV positive.	séropositif/ séropositive.	*sayrohpozeeteef/ sayrohpozeeteev*
I have ...	J'ai ...	*jay*
asthma.	de l'asthme.	*duh lasm*
MS.	la sclérose en plaques.	*la sklayrohz oñ plak*
high/low blood pressure.	une tension élevée basse.	*ewn toñsyawñ ayluhvay/bas*

I've ... myself.	Je me suis ...	*juh muh swee*
cut	coupé(e).	*koopay*
burnt	brûlé(e).	*brewlay*
I've been ...	J'ai été ...	*jay aytay*
bitten.	mordu(e).	*mordew*
stung.	piqué(e).	*peekay*
I can't ...	Je ne peux pas ...	*juh nuh puh pa*
move.	bouger.	*boojay*
feel my leg.	sentir ma jambe.	*soñteer ma joñb*
I have a broken tooth.	J'ai une dent cassée.	*jay ewn doñ kasay*
I've lost ...	J'ai perdu ...	*jay perdew*
a filling.	un plombage.	*uñ plawñbaj*
a crown.	une couronne.	*ewn kooron*

you may hear ...

Ça fait mal ici?	*sa fay mal eesee*	Does it hurt here?
C'est/Ce n'est pas grave.	*say/suh nay pa grav*	It's/It isn't serious.
C'est ...	*say(t)*	It's ...
une entorse.	*ewn oñtors*	a sprain.
une fracture.	*ewn fraktewr*	a fracture.
un claquage.	*uñ klakaj*	a pulled muscle.
une intoxication alimentaire.	*ewn añtokseekasyawñ aleemoñter*	food poisoning.
Il faut ...	*eel foh*	You need ...
opérer.	*opayray*	an operation.
aller à l'hôpital.	*alay a lopeetal*	to go to hospital.
faire une radiographie.	*fer ewn radyohgrafee*	to have an X-ray.
J'ai besoin d'un prélèvement de sang.	*jay buhzwañ duñ praylevmoñ duh soñ*	I need a blood sample.
Voilà une ordonnance.	*vwala ewn ordonoñs*	Here's a prescription.
Je vous mets un plombage (provisoire).	*juh voo me uñ plawñbaj (proveezwar)*	I'll put a (temporary) filling in.
Il faut arracher la dent.	*eel foh arashay la doñ*	I'll have to take the tooth out.

119

parts of the body

ankle	la cheville	*la shuveey*
arm	le bras	*luh bra*
back	le dos	*luh doh*
chest	la poitrine	*la pwatreen*
ear	l'oreille (f)	*lorey*
eye/eyes	l'œil/les yeux (m)	*luhy/layz yuh*
foot	le pied	*luh pyay*
hand	la main	*la mañ*
head	la tête	*la tet*
hips	les hanches	*lay oñsh*
kidneys	les reins	*lay rañ*
knee	le genou	*luh juhnoo*
leg	la jambe	*la joñb*
lung	le poumon	*luh poomawñ*
neck	le cou	*luh koo*
nose	le nez	*luh nay*
shoulder	l'épaule (f)	*aypohl*
tooth/teeth	la dent/les dents	*la doñ/lay doñ*
throat	la gorge	*la gorj*
tummy	le ventre/l'estomac	*luh voñtr/lestoma*
wrist	le poignet	*luh pwanye*

advice

you may hear ...

Prenez/Appliquez ...	*pruhnay/apleekay*	Take/Apply ...
ces cachets/ comprimés.	*say kashay/ kawñpreemay*	these tablets.
cette lotion.	*set lohsyawñ*	this lotion.
ce médicament.	*suh maydeekamoñ*	this medicine.
ces pilules.	*say peelewl*	these pills.
cette pommade.	*set pomad*	this ointment.
des suppositoires.	*day sewpozeetwar*	some suppositories.
du sirop.	*dew seeroh*	some cough mixture.
avant/après les repas	*avoñ/apre lay ruhpa*	before/after meals
avec de l'eau	*avek duh loh*	with water
à jeun	*a juñ*	on an empty stomach
une cuillerée	*ewn kweeuhray*	one spoonful
une fois/deux fois	*ewn fwa/duh fwa*	once/twice
par jour	*par joor*	a day
Ne pas prendre plus de trois fois par jour/en 24 heures.	*nuh pa proñdr plew duh trwa fwa par joor/oñ vañtkatr uhr*	Do not take more than three times a day/in 24 hours.
Risque de somnolence.	*reesk duh somnoloñs*	May cause drowsiness.
Avaler sans croquer.	*avalay soñ krokay*	Swallow whole.
Mâcher, ne pas avaler entier.	*mashay nuh paz avalay oñtyay*	Chew, do not swallow whole.
Ne pas utiliser près des yeux.	*nuh paz ewteeleezay pre dayz yuh*	Avoid contact with your eyes.
Il faut ...	*eel foh*	You must ...
rester au lit.	*restay oh lee*	stay in bed.
vous reposer.	*voo ruhpohzay*	rest.
boire beaucoup d'eau.	*bwar bohkoo doh*	drink lots of water.
Il ne faut pas ...	*eel nuh foh pa*	You mustn't ...
vous lever.	*voo luhvay*	get up.
courir.	*kooreer*	run.
faire des efforts.	*fer dayz efor*	take exercise.

check out 1

You're explaining your symptoms to the doctor.

○ J'ai vomi toute la nuit, j'ai mal à l'estomac.
  jay vomee toot la nwee jay mal a lestoma

- Ça fait mal ici?
  sa fay mal eesee

○ Oui! Et j'ai mal à la tête.
  wee. ay jay mal a la tet

- Qu'est-ce que vous avez mangé?
  keskuh vooz avay moñjay

○ Fruits de mer, poulet, gâteau à la crème.
  frwee duh mer poolay gatoh a la krem

- Mmm ... c'est une intoxication alimentaire. Il faut rester au lit et boire beaucoup d'eau.
  mmm ... sayt ewn añtoxeekasyawñ aleemoñter. eel foh restay oh lee ay bwar bohkoo doh

 What are the three main symptoms you describe?
What does the doctor tell you to do?

at the chemist's

you may say ...

I'd like something for ...	Je voudrais quelque chose ...	*juh voodray kelkuh shohz*
air/seasickness.	contre le mal de l'air/de mer.	*kawñtr luh mal duh ler/duh mer*
a sore throat.	pour le mal de gorge.	*poor luh mal duh gorj*
insect stings.	pour les piqûres d'insectes.	*poor lay peekewr dañsekt*
sunburn.	contre les coups de soleil.	*kawñtr lay koo duh soley*

122

I'd like a treatment sheet.	Je voudrais une feuille de soins.	*juh voodray ewn fuhy duh swañ*
I have an EHIC.	J'ai une CEAM.	*jay ewn say uh a em*
Do you have any ...	Vous avez ...	*vooz avay*
after-sun lotion?	une lotion après-soleil?	*ewn lohsyawñ apray soley*
aspirin?	de l'aspirine?	*duh laspeereen*
cough mixture?	du sirop?	*dew seeroh*
painkillers?	un analgésique?	*uñ nanaljayzeek*

Qu'est-ce que vous avez mangé/bu?	*keskuh vooz avay moñjay/bew*	What have you eaten/drunk?
Vous prenez déjà des médicaments?	*voo pruhnay dayja day maydeekamoñ*	Are you taking any other medicine?
Un paquet de six?	*uñ pakay duh sees*	A packet of six?

toiletries

condoms	les préservatifs	*lay prayzervateef*
deodorant	le déodorant	*luh dayodoroñ*
insect repellent	l'insecticide (m)	*lañsekteeseed*
nappies	les couches	*lay koosh*
plasters	les pansements adhésifs	*lay poñsmoñ adayzeef*
sanitary towels/ tampons	les serviettes hygiéniques/tampons	*lay servyet eejyayneek/tampawñ*
shampoo	le shampooing	*luh shoñpwañ*
soap	le savon	*luh savawñ*
sun lotion	la crème solaire	*la krem sohler*

car breakdown

you may say ...

I've broken down ...	Je suis en panne ...	*juh sweez oñ pan*
on the A10.	sur l'A10.	*sewr la dees*
ten kilometres from ...	à dix kilomètres de ...	*a dee keelohmetr duh*

The engine/The steering isn't working.	Le moteur/La direction ne marche pas.	*luh mohtuhr/la deereksyawñ nuh marsh pa*
The brakes aren't working.	Les freins ne marchent pas.	*lay frañ nuh marsh pa*
It won't start.	Elle ne démarre pas.	*el nuh daymar pa*
I've got a flat tyre.	J'ai un pneu crevé.	*jay uñ pnuh kruhvay*
The battery's flat.	La batterie est à plat.	*la batree ayt a pla*
I've run out of petrol.	J'ai une panne d'essence.	*jay ewn pan desoñs*
When will it be ready?	Ça sera prêt quand?	*sa suhra pre koñ*
How much will it cost?	Ça va coûter combien?	*sa va kootay kawñbyañ*

you may hear ...

Qu'est-ce qui ne va pas?	*keskee nuh va pas*	What's wrong?
Vous êtes où?	*vooz et oo*	Where are you?
Ne vous inquiétez pas.	*nuh vooz añkyaytay pa*	Don't worry.

car parts

accelerator	l'accélérateur (m)	*laxaylayratuhr*
battery	la batterie	*la batree*

124

bonnet	le capot	*luh kapoh*
brakes	les freins	*lay frañ*
bumper	le pare-choc	*luh par shok*
clutch	l'embrayage (m)	*loñbrayaj*
fan belt	la courroie de ventilateur	*la koorwa duh voñteelatuhr*
gearbox	la boîte de vitesses	*la bwat duh veetes*
headlights	les phares	*lay far*
lights	les feux	*lay fuh*
radiator	le radiateur	*luh radyatuhr*
steering wheel	le volant	*luh voloñ*
tyre	le pneu	*luh pnuh*
windscreen	le pare-brise	*luh par breez*
wipers	les essuie-glaces	*layz eswee glas*

check out 2

You've broken down on a main road, and a passing driver stops to help.

○ Pouvez-vous m'aider, Monsieur? Je suis en panne.
poovay voo mayday muhsyuh. juh sweez oñ pan

- Qu'est-ce qui ne va pas?
keskee nuh va pa

○ Je pense que c'est la courroie de ventilateur ...
juh poñs kuh say la koorwa duh voñteelatuhr

- Ne vous inquiétez pas, j'ai un câble de remorquage.
Il y a un garage à cinq minutes d'ici.
nuh vooz añkyaytay pa jay uñ kabl duh ruhmorkaj.
eelya uñ garaj a sañk meenewt deesee

(câble de remorquage = tow rope)

 What is the problem with the car?
What does the other driver offer to do?

125

theft or loss

you may say ...

I've lost ...	J'ai perdu ...	*jay perdew*
my wallet.	mon portefeuille.	*mawñ portuhfuhy*
my passport.	mon passeport.	*mawñ paspor*
my daughter.	ma fille.	*ma feey*
I've had ... stolen.	On m'a volé ...	*awñ ma volay*
my watch.	ma montre.	*ma mawñtr*
my bag.	mon sac.	*mawñ sak*
I've been ...	J'ai été ...	*jay aytay*
attacked.	attaqué(e).	*atakay*
mugged.	agressé(e).	*agresay*
raped.	violé(e).	*vyolay*
My car has been broken into.	On a forcé la porte de ma voiture.	*awñ na forsay la port duh ma vwatewr*
yesterday ...	hier ...	*eeyer*
morning	matin	*mataň*
afternoon	après-midi	*apraymeedee*
evening	soir	*swar*
this morning	ce matin	*suh mataň*
in ...	dans ...	*doñ(z)*
a shop	un magasin	*uñ magazaň*
the street	la rue	*la rew*

you may hear ...

Quelle couleur?	*kel kooluhr*	What colour is it?
Quelle heure?	*kel uhr*	What time?
Qu'est-ce qu'il y a dedans?	*keskeelya duhdoñ*	What's in it?
Vous l'avez perdu où?	*voo lavay perdew oo*	Where did you lose it?
Vous avez réalisé quand?	*vooz avay rayaleezay koñ*	When did you realize?

Quel est ...	kel ay	What's ...
votre nom/adresse?	votr nawñ/adres	your name/address?
votre numéro de passeport?	votr newmayroh duh paspor	your passport number?
le numéro d'immatriculation?	luh newmayroh deematreekew-lasyawñ	your car's registration number?
la marque de voiture?	la mark duh vwatewr	the make of your car?
Remplissez cette fiche.	roñpleesay set feesh	Fill in this form.
Revenez plus tard.	ruhvuhnay plew tar	Come back later.
Vous devez payer une amende.	voo duhvay payyay ewn amoñd	You have to pay a fine.

valuables

my briefcase	ma serviette	ma servyet
my (digital) camera	mon appareil-photo (numérique)	mawñ naparayfohtoh (newmayreek)
my driving licence	mon permis (de conduire)	mawñ permee (duh kawñdweer)
my handbag	mon sac à main	mawñ sak a mañ
my jewellery	mes bijoux	may beejoo
my laptop	mon ordinateur portable	mawñ nordeenatuhr portabl
my mobile	mon portable	mawñ portabl
some money	de l'argent	duh larjoñ
my MP3-player	mon lecteur mp3	mawñ lektuhr empaytrwa
my passport	mon passeport	mawñ paspor
my purse	mon porte-monnaie	mawñ portuhmonay
my rucksack	mon sac à dos	mawñ sak a doh
my suitcase	ma valise	ma valeez
my traveller's cheques	mes chèques de voyage/mes travellers	may shek duh vwiyaj/ may travluhr
my wallet	mon porte-feuille	mawñ portuhfuhy

check out 3

You've lost your handbag and go to the nearest police station.

○ J'ai perdu mon sac. Il est en cuir.
  jay perdew mawñ sak. eel ayt oñ kweer

- Quelle couleur?
  kel kooluhr

○ Marron et noir.
  marawñ ay nwar

- Qu'est-ce qu'il y a dedans?
  keskeelya duhdoñ

○ Il y a des travellers, de l'argent.
  eelya day travluhr duh larjoñ

Q What three words do you use to describe your bag?
   What valuables were inside?

sound check

These two groups of vowel sounds are ones you'll meet a lot in French:

eu and **œu**, pronounced a bit like the 'er' at the end of 'other' (though sometimes lengthened slightly):

yeux *yuh*   cœur *kuhr*   beurre *buhr*

ou or **oue**, which is usually an 'oo' sound:

jour *joor*   toux *too*

Practise by saying the following aloud:

les œufs *layz uh*	radiateur *radyatuhr*
feu *fuh*	fumeur *fewmuhr*
bouche *boosh*	coupé *koopay*
ouvert *oover*	couche *koosh*

try it out

a spoonful a day ...

Read the labels below and work out what you should or shouldn't do.

1 Deux cuillerées trois fois par jour avant les repas.
2 Prenez aux repas.
3 Ne pas prendre plus de quatre fois par jour.
4 Ne pas utiliser près des yeux.
5 Prenez à jeun.
6 Pour les enfants de plus de cinq ans.

as if you were there

You go to the chemist's to get something for your sore head. Follow the prompts below to play your part.

Bonjour, je peux vous aider?
(Say you've got a headache. Ask if they have any painkillers)
Vous êtes allergique à l'aspirine?
(Say no)
Voilà des comprimés. Un paquet de six ou un paquet de douze?
(Say a packet of twelve, please. Ask how much it is)

linkup

key phrases

Pouvez-vous m'aider?	**Can you** help me?
J'ai besoin de voir un docteur.	**I need** to see a doctor.
J'ai la diarrhée.	**I have** diarrhoea.
J'ai mal à la jambe.	**My** leg **hurts**.
Je suis constipé(e).	**I'm** constipated.
(Est-ce que) vous avez quelque chose pour le mal de gorge?	**Do you have anything for** a sore throat?
Le moteur **ne marche pas**.	The engine **isn't working**.
On m'a volé mon passeport.	**I've had** my passport **stolen**.
J'ai perdu mon portefeuille.	**I've lost** my wallet.

possession

Similarly to adjectives, the word for 'my' changes, depending on the word that follows:

J'ai perdu **mon** sac. I've lost my bag. (it's **le** sac)

J'ai perdu **ma** valise. I've lost my suitcase. (it's **la** valise)

Mes enfants ont le mal de mer. My children are seasick/have seasickness. (it's **les** enfants)

Note that it's the gender of the thing you possess that determines whether you use mon, ma or mes, not whether you are male or female.

For more about possessives, see the Language Builder, p135.

Instead of using an apostrophe to talk about things belonging to someone or something else, French uses de (of):

la valise de mon père my father's suitcase (literally, the suitcase of my father)

Language **Builder**

gender

All nouns in French (words for objects, people or abstract concepts) are either masculine or feminine. Masculine nouns are preceded by le or un (meaning 'the' or 'a'), and it's la or une for feminine nouns:

le livre the book   un sac de farine a bag of flour
la pharmacie the chemist   une salade verte a green salad

There's no clear-cut logic to which words are masculine and which are feminine, so just try to learn by heart the gender of any new word you meet. However, the spelling often gives some clues:
most nouns ending in -age, -ment or -oir are masculine;
most nouns ending in -ance, -ence, -té and -ion are feminine.

Some nouns – usually relating to people – have two forms, masculine and feminine:

un serveur a waiter   un ami a male friend
une serveuse a waitress   une amie a female friend

The gender of a noun is important because it affects other words like 'from' and 'some' that come before the noun, as well as words used to describe it (adjectives). However, if you get the gender wrong you'll usually still be understood.

'a' & 'the': articles

	masculine	feminine	plural
a	un	une	
the	le	la	les

Some examples:

un journal a newspaper   une voiture a car
le magasin the shop   la pomme the apple
les chaussures the shoes

Before a vowel or silent h, both le and la change to l':

l'église the church   l'hôpital the hospital

Nouns in the plural change their endings. Usually, this just means a silent 's' is added.

une voiture, deux voiture**s** a car, two cars

some, any, from, of

In French de is used for all these words, but sometimes it changes to show gender and plurals. This is how:

- feminine nouns: de + la:
  de la confiture some jam
- before a vowel and h (for both genders): de + l':
  de l'eau some water le nom de l'hôtel the hotel name
- masculine nouns: de + le = du:
  le devant du magasin the front of the shop
- plural (for both genders): de + les = des:
  des chaussures some shoes

Here's how you might say:
'some': Je voudrais **de la** limonade. I'd like some lemonade.
'any': Avez-vous **des** pommes? Have you got any apples?
'from': Je viens **de** Londres. I come from London.
If you just want to say 'of' (for example, to ask for a particular quantity of something), it's simply de:
un demi-kilo **de** tomates half a kilo of tomatoes
une bouteille **de** vin a bottle of wine

questions

You can ask a question by simply raising your intonation at the end of a statement:
Vous voulez une orange? Do you want an orange?
Another way is to change the word order:
Voulez-vous une orange? Do you want an orange?
Or add Est-ce que ... to the beginning:
Est-ce que vous voulez une orange? Do you want an orange?

To ask a 'What ...?' question, add Qu'est-ce que ...? to a statement:
Qu'est-ce que je fais? What do I do?
Qu'est-ce qu'elle demande? What's she asking?

If you want to ask a 'What is/What are ...?' question, or ask about a noun, then you can use quel (or quelle for feminine words):
Quel est le prix? What is the price?

When the noun is plural, you'll need to add an s:
Quel**s** sandwichs avez-vous? What sandwiches have you got?

An easy alternative way to ask that question is:
Qu'est-ce que vous avez comme sandwichs? What sandwiches have you got?

negatives

To make a sentence negative in French, you wrap ne ... pas round the verb:
Je **ne** suis **pas** français. I am not French.
Ça **ne** va **pas**! It's not all right!/I'm not well.
Je **ne** comprends **pas**. I don't understand.

Before a vowel, ne becomes n':
Je **n'**ai **pas** de monnaie. I don't have any change.
Il **n'**est **pas** à la maison. He's not at home.

When you want to express other negative concepts (like 'nothing', 'no one' or 'never'), you replace pas with different words:
Il **ne** reste **plus** de pommes. There are **no more** apples left.
Je **ne** roule **jamais** vite. I **never** drive fast.
Je **ne** vois **rien**. I see **nothing**/I **don't** see **anything**.
Il **n'**y a **personne**. There is **nobody** there.
Il **n'**y a **ni** bus **ni** train. There are **neither** buses **nor** trains.
Je **n'**ai **que** dix euros. I **only** have ten euros.

In spoken French, the ne part of a negative is often left out:
C'est **pas** grave. It doesn't matter.

adjectives

Words that describe something or someone (adjectives) always agree with the noun they're describing, which means they have different endings for masculine and feminine.

Most adjectives can be made feminine simply by adding an -e:
un petit appartement a small flat
une petit**e** fille a little girl
un livre intéressant an interesting book
Elle est très intelligent**e**. She's very intelligent.
The extra -e usually changes the way the word sounds too, as the last consonant is heard instead of being silent.

Adjectives also change if the word they describe is plural – most of them simply take an -s, which is usually silent:
des chaussettes bleue**s** blue socks
les petit**s** gâteaux little cakes

Unlike in English, French adjectives usually come after the noun they describe:
une auto **rouge** a red car   un melon **mûr** a ripe melon

Some of the more common ones, however, always go before, including those listed in the table below.

adjective	masculine	feminine
small	petit	petite
tall/large	grand	grande
young	jeune	jeune
old	vieux/vieil	vieille
pretty	joli	jolie
beautiful	beau/bel	belle
good	bon	bonne
bad	mauvais	mauvaise
big	gros	grosse
excellent	excellent	excellente
short	court	courte
kind	gentil	gentille
new	nouveau	nouvelle

Ordinal numbers also come before the noun:
C'est la deuxième rue à gauche. It's the second street on the left.

possession

To show possession in French, use de:
le chien **de** David David**'s** dog
la maison **de** ma mère My mother**'s** house

There are words to mean 'my', 'his', 'their', etc, as listed at the top of p135. These change according to the gender of the item possessed, **not** the gender of the owner.

Language **Builder**

	masculine	feminine	plural
my	mon	ma	mes
your	ton	ta	tes
his/her/its	son	sa	ses
our	notre	notre	nos
your	votre	votre	vos
their	leur	leur	leurs

The plural is the same for masculine and feminine nouns:
nos fils our sons   nos filles our daughters
Ma chemise est verte et mes yeux sont bleus. My shirt is green
and my eyes are blue.
Votre robe est très jolie. Your dress is very pretty.

this, that, these

These words behave like adjectives, agreeing with the noun in
gender and in number (singular or plural).
masculine: ce melon this melon   ces melons these melons
feminine: cette table this table   ces tables these tables

If you just want to point out an object it's much easier to use ça:
Je voudrais ça! I'd like that!

talking to people

In French, there are two ways of saying 'you' – vous and tu – a
more formal and an informal version. Most of the language you'll
need or hear when in France will involve the polite vous, used
when talking to strangers or someone you don't know very well:
Est-ce que **vous avez** un guide en anglais? Do you have a
guidebook in English?
Vous aimez l'opéra? Do you like opera?

You also use vous when addressing more than one person.

Between young people, friends or family, or to a child, use tu:
Est-ce que **tu as** de la monnaie? Do you have any change?
Tu aimes jouer au tennis? Do you like playing tennis?

Remember to use the correct ending of the verb for each form. If in doubt, use vous. And when someone suggests you call him or her tu (On se tutoie?) you know you've made a friend!

the word *on*

This is something you'll hear a lot in France. It can be used to refer to people in general, in much the same way that English would use the words 'they', 'you' or 'people' (and it's by no means as formal or stilted as 'one'). For example:

En France, **on** mange des escargots. In France, **they** eat snails.
On dit que c'est difficile. **People** say that it's difficult.
On n'a pas besoin de billet. **You** don't need a ticket.

It's also used in conversation instead of nous ('we'):
On y va? Shall **we** go?
On cherche la banque. **We**'re looking for the bank.
On peut avoir l'addition? Can **we** have the bill?

verbs

The endings of French verbs change according to who does the action and when. What's more, the present tense in French can be used to mean both 'I speak' and 'I am speaking'.

Most infinitives (the part of the verb you'll find in a dictionary) end in -er, e.g. parler – to speak. To use regular verbs ending in -er in their present tense, you simply remove the last two letters and add the relevant ending, as follows:
je parl**e** I speak (or I'm speaking)
tu parl**es** you speak (informal)
il/elle parl**e** he/she/it speaks
nous parl**ons** we speak
vous parl**ez** you speak (formal or plural)
ils/elles parl**ent** they speak

Other infinitives end in -ir or -re instead and there are similar rules to help you form the different endings. Some verbs, however, do not follow a set pattern, so the way they change must be learnt separately. Some of the most useful irregular verbs are shown on p137.

Language **Builder**

aller – to go	
je vais	I go
tu vas	you go
il/elle va	he/she/it goes
nous allons	we go
vous allez	you go
ils/elles vont	they go

avoir – to have	
j'ai	I have
tu as	you have
il/elle a	he/she/it has
nous avons	we have
vous avez	you have
ils/elles ont	they have

être – to be	
je suis	I am
tu es	you are
il/elle est	he/she/it is
nous sommes	we are
vous êtes	you are
ils/elles sont	they are

faire – to make/do	
je fais	I do
tu fais	you do
il/elle fait	he/she/it does
nous faisons	we do
vous faites	you do
ils/elles font	they do

vouloir – to want	
je/tu veux	I/you want
il/elle veut	he/she/it wants
nous voulons	we want
vous voulez	you want
ils/elles veulent	they want

Answers

Bare Necessities ......

check out
1 on the right; €3.70
2 he says you speak French well; you are asked how you are and what you do for a living
3 false, it's £40; £1 = €1.40

know-how
1 Bonne nuit, à demain!
2 Je suis gallois(e), je viens de Cardiff.
3 Vous voulez prendre un verre?
4 J'ai quarante-cinq ans et j'ai trois enfants.

match it up
1b 2d 3a 4f 5c 6e

time flies ...
1 Il est trois heures moins le quart.
2 Le magasin ferme à dix-neuf heures quinze.
3 Le train va partir dans vingt-cinq minutes.
4 Jusqu'à midi et quart.
5 Ma femme arrive à dix heures dix.

as if you were there
Bonjour (Monsieur), ça va, merci. Et vous?
bawñjoor (muhsuyh) sa va mersee. ay voo
Oui, je suis de Londres.
wee juh swee duh lawñdr
Je m'appelle Katherine.
juh mapel katreen

Getting Around ....

check out
1 false, it's the first road on the right
2 unlimited mileage and insurance are included; she asks for the driver's licence
3 unleaded petrol; false, he warns you there's a toll (un péage) on the motorway
4 a) false – you must change at Nice; b) false – it leaves at 14.28; c) true

picture this
1g 2d 3f 4b 5a 6c 7e

mind the gap
1 Il faut
2 pont
3 voudrais ... gasoil/gazole
4 peux louer ... vélo
5 aller simple

as if you were there
Pardon (Monsieur), il y a une station-service près d'ici?
pardawñ (muhsuhr) eelya ewn stasyawñ desoñs pre deesee
Merci, et pour aller à l'autoroute?
mersee ay poor alay a lohtohroot

Somewhere to Stay ....

check out
1 double and single rooms; false
2 true; in the restaurant on the ground floor, from 6.30am
3 a tent; €21
4 €450; true

match it up

1c 2f 3e 4b 5a 6d

mind the gap

1 complet 2 cher 3 combien
4 chambre 5 caravane
6 climatisation

as if you were there

Bonjour, je voudrais une chambre.
bawñjoor juh voodray ewn shoñbr

Pour deux.
poor duh
La chambre à grand lit, s'il vous plaît.
la shoñbr a groñ lee seelvooplay
Pour trois nuits. C'est combien par nuit?
poor trwa nwee. say kawñbyañ par nwee
Le petit déjeuner est compris?
luh puhtee dayjuhnay ay kawñpree

Buying Things ....

check out

1 €22; slices
2 they've sold out; strawberries
3 size 42; by credit card
4 2nd floor; over there, next to the toys

question time

1c 2b 3a

as if you were there

Bonjour, je voudrais ça; qu'est-ce que c'est?
bawñjoor juh voodray sa keskuh say
Bon! J'en voudrais une autre, s'il vous plaît. C'est combien?
bawñ. joñ voodray ewn ohtr seelvooplay. say kawñbyañ

Café Life...................

check out

1 cheese, ham, ham salad sandwiches; a beer and an apple juice
2 a large coffee with cream, a lager, a glass of white wine and a freshly squeezed lemon juice

odd one out

1 jus de raisin (the others are snacks)
2 un grand crème (the others are alcoholic drinks)
3 une salade composée (the others are sweet)

as if you were there

Je voudrais un citron pressé, sans glaçons, un thé au lait et un verre de vin blanc.
juh voodray uñ seetrawñ presay soñ glasawñ uñ tay oh lay ay uñ ver duh vañ bloñ
Qu'est-ce que vous avez comme sandwichs?
keskuh vooz avay kom soñdweetsh
Je voudrais un sandwich au thon et une glace au chocolat.
juh voodray uñ soñdweetsh oh tawñ ay ewn glas oh shokohla

Answers

Eating Out ....

check out

1 €19; half a bottle of rosé wine
2 You still haven't been served your wine; your steak is very tough; your knife is dirty – you ask for another.

match it up

1b 2c 3c

as if you were there

Je voudrais les artichauts et les moules, s'il vous plaît, et une salade verte.
juh voodray layz arteeshoh ay lay mool seelvooplay ay ewn salad vert

Un verre de vin blanc, s'il vous plaît.
uñ ver duh vañ bloñ seelvooplay

Entertainment ....

check out

1 The assistant mentions boat trips, museums, an amusement park and painting exhibitions.
2 no
3 waterskiing; €30 for half an hour

mind the gap

1 des chaises longues
2 des billets
3 une raquette
4 des rames
5 un feu d'artifice

as if you were there

Bonjour, je voudrais un guide du musée en anglais.
bawñjoor juh voodray uñ geed dew mewzay oñ noñglay

Merci. Ça fait combien?
mersee. sa fay kawñbyañ

Emergencies ....

check out

1 You've been sick all night, you have stomach ache and your head aches; he says you should stay in bed and drink lots of water.
2 You think it's the fan belt; he offers to tow you to the nearest garage (five minutes away).
3 leather, brown and black; traveller's cheques and money

a spoonful a day ...

1 Take two spoonfuls, three times a day, before meals.
2 Take with food.
3 Don't take more than four times a day.
4 Don't use near eyes.
5 Take on an empty stomach.
6 For children over the age of 5.

as if you were there

J'ai mal à la tête. Vous avez un analgésique?
jay mal a la tet. vooz avay uñ nanaljayzeek

Non.
nawñ

Un paquet de douze, s'il vous plaît. Ça fait combien?
uñ pakay duh dooz seelvooplay. sa fay kawñbyañ

(v.) = verb; (m) = masculine;
(f) = feminine; (pl) = plural

A

a un(e) *uñ/ewn*
abcess abcès, l' (m) *abse*
about (approx.) environ *oñveerawñ*
accelerator accélérateur, l' (m)
 axaylayratuhr
ache mal, le *mal*
add (v.) ajouter *ajootay*
address adresse, l' (f) *adres*
adult adulte, l' (m/f) *adewlt*
advise (v.) conseiller *kawñsayyay*
aeroplane avion, l' (m) *avyawñ*
after après *apre*
afternoon après-midi, l' (m/f)
 apremeedee
again encore *oñkor*
against contre *kawñtr*
agency agence, l' (f) *ajoñs*
air air, l' (m) *er*
air conditioning climatisation, la
 kleemateezasyawñ
airport aéroport, l' (m) *aayropor*
alcoholic alcoolisé(e) *alkoleezay*
all tout(e)/tous (mpl)/toutes (fpl)
 too/toot/too/toot
allergic allergique *alerjeek*
ambulance ambulance, l' (f) *oñbewloñs*
amusement attraction, l' (f) *atraksyawñ*
and et *ay*
animal animal, l' (m) *aneemal*
ankle cheville, la *shuhveey*
antibiotics antibiotique, l' (m)
 oñteebyoteek
any du (m)/de la (f)/des (mpl/fpl)
 dew/de la/day
apartment appartement, l' (m)
 apartuhmoñ
aperitif apéritif, l' (m) *apayreetif*
appendicitis appendicite, l' (f)
 apañdeeseet
appetite appétit, l' (m) *apaytee*
apply (v.) appliquer *apleekay*
appointment rendez-vous, le *roñdayvoo*
arm bras, le *bra*
armband flotteur, le *flotuhr*
art art, l' (m) *ar*
as comme *kom*
ashtray cendrier, le *soñdreeay*
aspirin aspirine, l' (f) *aspeereen*
asthma asthme, l' (m) *asm*
at à *a*
at once tout de suite *tooduhsweet*
at the au (m)/à la (f)/aux (mpl/fpl)
 oh/ala/oh
avocado avocat, l' (m) *avohka*

B

back dos, le *doh*
bad mauvais(e) *mohve/mohvez*
badly mal *mal*
bag sac, le *sak*
bakery boulangerie, la *booloñjree*
balcony balcon, le *balkawñ*
ball (small; large) balle, la; ballon, le
 bal; balawñ
ballet ballet, le *balay*
bank banque, la *boñk*
banknote billet, le *beeyay*
bar bar, le *bar*
bar (chocolate) plaquette, la *plaket*
basement sous-sol, le *soosol*
basket corbeille, la *korbayy*
bath bain, le *bañ*
bathroom salle de bains, la *sal duh bañ*
bathtub baignoire, la *baynywar*
battery (car) batterie, la *batree*
battery (e.g. torch) pile, la *peel*
beach plage, la *plaj*
beautiful beau/belle *boh/bel*
beauty beauté, la *bohtay*
bed lit, le *lee*
bedroom chambre, la *shoñbr*
before avant *avoñ*
behind derrière *deryer*
belt ceinture, la *sañtewr*
(fan) belt courroie (de ventilateur), la
 koorwa (duh voñteelatuhr)
bench banc, le *boñ*
bicycle vélo, le *vayloh*
bidet bidet, le *beeday*
big gros/grosse *groh/grohs*
bill addition, l' (f); note, la *adeesyawñ/not*
bin poubelle, la *poobel*
biscuit biscuit, le *beeskwee*
black noir(e) *nwar*
blanket couverture, la *koovertewr*
bleach eau de Javel, l' (f) *oh duh javel*
blind (sight-impaired) aveugle *avuhgl*
blinds stores, les (mpl) *stor*
blister ampoule, l' (f) *oñpool*
blond blond(e) *blawñ/blawñd*
blood sang, le *soñ*
blood pressure tension, la *toñsyawñ*
blouse chemisier, le *shuhmeezyay*
blue bleu(e) *bluh*
board (plank) planche, la *ploñsh*
boat bateau, le *batoh*
boiler chaudière, la *shohdyer*
bone os, l' (m) *os*
book (reading) livre, le *leevr*
bookshop librairie, la *leebrayree*
boss patron, le/patronne, la *patrawñ/patron*

bottle bouteille, la *bootayy*
box boîte, la *bwat*
box (theatre) loge, la *loj*
boy garçon, le *garsawñ*
brake frein, le *frañ*
brand marque, la *mark*
brand new neuf/neuve *nuhf/nuhv*
brandy cognac, le; eau-de-vie, l' (f)
  konyak; oh duh vee
bread pain, le *pañ*
break into (v.) forcer *forsay*
breakdown panne, la *pan*
breakdown service dépannage, le
  daypanaj
bridge pont, le *pawñ*
briefcase serviette, la *servyet*
bring (v.) apporter *aportay*
British britannique *breetaneek*
broken cassé(e) *kasay*
broken down en panne *oñ pan*
bronchitis bronchite, la *brawñsheet*
brooch broche, la *brosh*
brown brun(e); marron *bruñ/brewn;*
  marawñ
bumper pare-chocs, le *par shok*
bungee jumping saut à l'élastique, le
  soh a laylasteek
buoy/rubber ring bouée, la *booay*
burn brûlure, la *brewlewr*
burnt brûlé(e) *brewlay*
bus bus, le; car, le *bews; kar*
busy occupé(e) *okewpay*
but mais *may*
butcher's shop boucherie, la *booshree*
buttock fesse, la *fes*
buy (v.) acheter *ashtay*
by par *par*

C

cable car téléphérique, le *taylayfayreek*
cake gâteau, le *gatoh*
cake shop/cakes pâtisserie, la *patisree*
call appel, l' (m) *apel*
call (v.) appeler *aplay*
camcorder caméscope, le *kamayskop*
camera appareil-photo, l' (m) *aparayfohtoh*
camp (v.) camper *koñpay*
camping camping, le *koñpeeng*
campsite terrain de camping, le *terañ duh*
  koñpeeng
can (e.g. of lemonade) boîte, la *bwat*
candle bougie, la *boojee*
car voiture, la *vwatewr*
carafe carafe, la *karaf*
caravan caravane, la *karavan*
card carte, la *kart*
cardboard carton, le *kartawñ*
carnival carnaval, le *karnaval*

carry on (v.) continuer *kawñteeneway*
carton carton, le *kartawñ*
cash espèces (fpl) *espes*
cashpoint distributeur automatique de
  billets, le *deestreebewtuhr ohtomateek*
  duh beeyay
castle château, le *shatoh*
central heating chauffage central, le
  shohfaj soñtral
chair chaise, la *shayz*
chalet chalet, le *shalay*
championship championnat, le *shoñpyona*
change (v.) changer *shoñjay*
(small) change monnaie, la *monay*
changing room (in pool) vestiaire, la
  vestyer
checkout, till caisse, la *kes*
cheese fromage, le *fromaj*
chemist's shop pharmacie, la *farmasee*
cheque chèque, le *shek*
chest/bust poitrine, la *pwatreen*
chestnut marron, le *marawñ*
chicken pox varicelle, la *vareesel*
child enfant, l' (m/f) *oñfoñ*
Christmas Noël *nohel*
church église, l' (f) *aygleez*
circle (in theatre) balcon, le *balkawñ*
circus cirque, le *seerk*
city wall rempart, le *roñpar*
classical classique *klaseek*
cloakroom (e.g. in theatre) vestiaire, le
  vestyer
close (v.) fermer *fermay*
clothes vêtements, les (mpl) *vetmoñ*
club club, le *kluhb*
clutch embrayage, l' (m) *oñbrayaj*
coach car, le *kar*
coast côte, la *koht*
coat manteau, le *moñtoh*
coathanger cintre, le *sañtr*
cocoa cacao, le *kakaoh*
cod cabillaud, le *kabeeyoh*
coke (drink) coca, le *kohka*
cold (temperature) froid(e) *frwa(d)*
cold (medical complaint) rhume, le *rewm*
cold meat charcuterie, la *sharkewtree*
collarbone clavicule, la *klaveekewl*
colour couleur, la *kooluhr*
come (v.) venir *vuhneer*
come back (v.) revenir *ruhvuhneer*
commission commission, la *komeesyawñ*
computing informatique, l' (f) *añformateek*
concert concert, le *kawñser*
concession réduction, la *raydewksyawñ*
concussion commotion cérébrale, la
  komohsyawñ sayraybral
condom préservatif, le *prayzervateef*
connection correspondance, la

korespawñdoñs

constipated constipé(e) *kawñsteepay*

contact lenses lentilles de contact, les (fpl) *loñteey duh kawñtakt*

contagious contagieux/contagieuse *kawñtajuh/kawñtajuhz*

continue (v.) continuer *kawñteeneway*

cooker cuisinière, la *kweezeenyer*

cooking cuisine, la *kweezeen*

cool frais/fraîche *fre/fresh*

copy (e.g. photo) double, le *doobl*

cork bouchon, le *booshawñ*

corkscrew tire-bouchon, le *teer booshawñ*

corner coin, le *kwañ*

cottage chalet, le; gîte, le *shalay; jeet*

cotton coton, le *kotawñ*

cough toux, la *too*

counter guichet, le *geeshay*

country pays, le *payy*

countryside campagne, la *la kowñpany*

course (over time) cours, le *koor*

covered market halles, les (f) *al*

craft workshop atelier, l' (m) *atuhlyay*

cream crème, la *krem*

credit crédit, le *kraydee*

cross (v.) traverser *traversay*

crossing traversée, la *traversay*

crossroads carrefour, le *karfoor*

crown couronne, la *kooron*

cup tasse, la; coupe, la (sport) *tas; koop*

current courant, le *koorawñ*

curtain rideau, le *reedoh*

customers clientèle, la *kleeoñtel*

cut coupé(e) *koopay*

cyclist cycliste, le/la *seekleest*

D

dairy products produits laitiers, les (mpl) *prodwee laytyay*

dark (colour) foncé(e) *fawñsay*

date (day) date, la *dat*

daughter fille, la *feey*

day jour, le *joor*

(the) day before yesterday avant-hier *avoñtyer*

dead end impasse, l' (f) *añpas*

deaf sourd(e) *soor/soord*

dear cher/chère *sher*

deckchair chaise longue, la *shayz lawñg*

deep profond(e) *prohfawñ/prohfawñd*

delicatessen traiteur, le *traytuhr*

delicious délicieux/délicieuse *dayleesyuh/dayleesyuhz*

delighted enchanté(e) *oñshoñtay*

dentist dentiste, le/la *doñteest*

department (in shop) rayon, le *rayawñ*

deposit caution, la *kohsyawñ*

depth profondeur, la *prohfawñduhr*

dessert dessert, le *deser*

develop (v.) développer *dayvuhlopay*

diabetic diabétique *dyabayteek*

diarrhoea diarrhée, la *deearay*

digital camera appareil-photo numérique, l' (m) *aparayfohtoh newmayreek*

dinghy canot, le *kanoh*

dining room salle à manger, la *sal a moñjay*

dipped lights codes, les (mpl) *kod*

direction direction, la *deereksyawñ*

dish plat, le (on menu); coupe, la (for ice cream or fruit) *pla; koop*

disposable camera appareil-photo jetable, l' (m) *aparayfohtoh juhtabl*

disturb (v.) déranger *dayroñjay*

diving plongée, la *plawñjay*

DIY bricolage, le *breekohlaj*

dizziness vertige, le *verteej*

do (v.) faire *fer*

doctor médecin, le *maydsañ*

door porte, la *port*

door (train/car) portière, la *portyer*

dozen douzaine, la *doozen*

draught beer pression, la *presyawñ*

dress robe, la *rob*

dressing (medical) pansement, le *poñsmoñ*

drink boisson, la *bwasawñ*

drink (v.) boire *bwar*

drinking (water) (eau) potable *(oh) potabl*

drive (v.) conduire *kawñdweer*

drowsiness somnolence, la *somnohloñs*

drums (music) batterie, la *batree*

dubbed foreign film version française, la *versyawñ froñsez*

dustbin poubelle, la *poobel*

E

ear oreille, l' (f) *orey*

ear infection otite, l' (f) *ohteet*

earring boucle d'oreille, la *bookluh dorey*

east est, l' (m) *est*

eat (v.) manger *moñjay*

effort effort, l' (m) *efor*

egg œuf, l' (m) *uhf*

eggs œufs, les (mpl) *uh*

electricity électricité, l' (f) *aylektreeseetay*

English anglais(e) *oñglay/oñglez*

English Channel Manche, la *moñsh*

enough assez *asay*

enter (v.) entrer *oñtray*

entertainment distractions, les (fpl) *deestraksyawn*

epilepsy épilepsie, l' (f) *aypeelepsee*

epileptic épileptique *aypeelepteek*

errand course, la *koors*

escalator escalier roulant, l' (m) *eskalyay rooloñ*

estate agency agence immobilière, l' (f) *ajoñs eemohbeelyer*

even même *mem*

evening soir, le *swar*

everything tout *too*

excellent excellent(e) *exeloñ/exeloñt*

exchange change, le *shoñj*

excuse (v.) excuser *exkewzay*

exhaust (car) échappement, l' (m) *ayshapmoñ*

exhibition exposition, l' (f) *expohzeesyawñ*

exit sortie, la *sortee*

expensive cher/chère *sher*

extra en supplément; en sus *oñ sewplaymoñ; oñ sews*

extract (v.) arracher *arashay*

eye œil, l' (m) *uhy*

eyes yeux, les (mpl) *yuh*

F

factory usine, l' (f) *ewzeen*

fair (event) foire, la; fête, la *fwar; fet*

fairly (quite) assez *asay*

far loin *lwañ*

farm ferme, la *ferm*

fee redevance, la *ruhduhvoñs*

feel (v.) sentir *soñteer*

festival festival, le *festeeval*

festivity fête, la *fet*

fever température, la; fièvre, la *toñpayratewr; fyayvr*

field champ, le *shoñ*

fill (v.) remplir *roñpleer*

fill up (petrol) (v.) faire le plein *fer luh plañ*

film (camera) pellicule, la *peleekewl*

filter filtre, le *feeltr*

find (v.) trouver *troovay*

finish (v.) finir *feeneer*

fire feu, le *fuh*

fireworks feu d'artifice, le *fuh darteefees*

fish poisson, le *pwasawñ*

fishing pêche, la *pesh*

fizzy gazeux/gazeuse *gazuh/gazuhz*

fizzy orange orangeade, l' (f) *oroñjad*

flavour (e.g. ice cream) parfum, le *parfañ*

flight vol, le *vol*

flipper palme, la *palm*

floor (storey) étage, l' (m) *aytaj*

flour farine, la *fareen*

flow cours, le *koor*

'flu (influenza) grippe, la *greep*

fly (v.) voler *volay*

foot pied, le *pyay*

football foot(ball), le *foot(bohl)*

for pour; depuis *poor; duhpwee*

forbidden interdit(e); défense de *añterdee/añterdeet; dayfoñs duh*

force (v.) forcer *forsay*

forget (v.) oublier *oobleeay*

form fiche, la *feesh*

fracture fracture, la *fraktewr*

free libre *leebr*

free of charge gratuit(e) *gratwee/gratweet*

French français(e) *froñsay/froñsez*

French stick baguette, la; ficelle, la; flûte, la *baget; feesel; flewt*

fresh frais/fraîche *fre/fresh*

from de; à partir de (with times and dates) *duh; a parteer duh*

frozen food surgelés, les (mpl) *sewrjuhlay*

fruit fruit, le *frwee*

full plein(e); complet/complète *plañ/plen; kawñple/kawñplet*

full board pension complète, la *poñsyawñ kawñplet*

function (v.) marcher *marshay*

funfair fête foraine, la *fet foren*

G

gallery galerie, la *galree*

garage garage, le *garaj*

garden jardin, le *jardañ*

garnished garni(e) *garnee*

gas gaz, le *gaz*

gear (in car) vitesse, la *veetes*

gear box boîte de vitesses, la *bwat duh veetes*

general général(e) *jaynayral*

general practitioner, GP généraliste, le *jaynayraleest*

get off (bus, etc.) (v.) descendre *desoñdr*

gift cadeau, le *kadoh*

gift-wrapped parcel paquet-cadeau, le *pakay-kadoh*

girl fille, la *feey*

give the exact money (on bus) faire l'appoint *fer lapwañ*

give way cédez (le passage) *sayday (luh pasaj)*

glacier glacier, le *glasyay*

glass verre, le *ver*

glasses lunettes, les (fpl) *lewnet*

glossy brillant(e) *breeyoñ/breeyoñt*

gluten-free sans gluten *soñ glewten*

go (v.) aller *alay*

go away (v.) partir *parteer*

go down (v.) descendre *desoñdr*

go out (v.) sortir *sorteer*

goblet coupe, la *koop*
golf golf, le *golf*
golf course terrain de golf, le *terañ duh golf*
good bon/bonne; bien *bawñ/bon; byañ*
good evening bonsoir *bawñswar*
ground (e.g. football) terrain, le *terañ*
green vert(e) *ver/vert*
grey gris(e) *gree/greez*
grocer's shop alimentation générale, l' (f); épicerie, l' (f) *aleemoñtasyawñ jaynayral; aypeesree*
ground floor rez-de-chaussée, le *ray duh shohsay*
guest hôte, l' (m/f); invité(e), l' (m/f) *oht; añveetay*
guest house pension, la *poñsyawñ*
guide (person) guide, le *geed*
guidebook guide, le *geed*

H

hairdressing coiffure, la *kwafewr*
hairstyle coiffure, la *kwafewr*
half demi(e), le/la; moitié, la *duhmee; mwatyay*
half an hour demi-heure, la *duhmee uhr*
half board demi-pension, la *duhmee poñsyawñ*
half-pint (of beer) demi, le *duhmee*
ham jambon, le *joñbawñ*
hand main, la *mañ*
handkerchief mouchoir, le *mooshwar*
hangover gueule de bois, la *guhl duh bwa*
harbour port, le *por*
hard dur(e) *dewr*
hardware (store) quincaillerie, la *kañkiyree*
have (v.) avoir *avwar*
have a pain (v.) avoir mal *avwar mal*
head tête, la *tet*
headlight phare, le *far*
health food shop magasin de produits diététiques, le *magazañ duh prodwee dyaytayteek*
heart cœur, le *kuhr*
heartburn brûlures d'estomac, les (fpl) *brewlewr destoma*
heating chauffage, le *shohfaj*
heavy lourd(e) *loor/loord*
heavy goods vehicle poids lourd, le *pwa loor*
hello bonjour *bawñjoor*
help! au secours! *oh suhkoor*
help (v.) aider *ayday*
helpful aimable *aymabl*
herbal tea infusion, l' (f); tisane, la *añfewzyawñ; teezan*

here ici *eesee*
here it is voilà *vwala*
high haut(e) *oh/oht*
high chair chaise haute, la *shayz oht*
hiking randonnée pédestre, la *roñdonay paydestr*
hire (v.) louer *looay*
hire, hiring location, la *lohkasyawñ*
HIV-positive séropositif/séropositive *sayrohpozeeteef/sayrohpozeeteev*
holidays vacances, les (fpl) *vakoñs*
homemade maison *mayzawñ*
horse cheval, le *shuhval*
horseriding équitation, l' (f) *aykeetasyawñ*
hospital hôpital, l' (m) *opeetal*
host hôte, l' (m) *oht*
hot chaud(e) *shoh/shohd*
hotel hôtel, l' (m) *ohtel*
hour heure, l' (f) *uhr*
house maison, la *mayzawñ*
household ménager/ménagère *maynajay/maynajer*
how comment *komoñ*
how much; how many combien *kawñbyañ*
husband mari, le *maree*

I

I je *juh*
I have j'ai *jay*
ice glace, la *glas*
ice cream glace, la *glas*
ice cream parlour glacier, le *glasyay*
ice cube glaçon, le *glasawñ*
ice rink patinoire, la *pateenwar*
iced (coffee) frappé(e) *frapay*
in dans; en *doñ; oñ*
in a hurry pressé(e) *presay*
in front of devant *duhvoñ*
in order to pour *poor*
included inclus(e); compris(e) *añklew/ añklewz; kawñpree/kawñpreez*
indigestion indigestion, l' (f) *añdeejestyawñ*
infection infection, l' (f) *añfexyawñ*
inflatable pneumatique *pnuhmateek*
injection piqûre, la *peekewr*
inn auberge, l' (f) *ohberj*
insect insecte, l' (m) *añsekt*
inside dedans *duhdoñ*
insurance assurance, l' (f) *asewroñs*
interesting intéressant(e) *añtayresoñ/añtayresoñt*
internet café cybercafé, le *seeberkafay*
internet connection connexion internet, la *konexyawñ añternet*

interval (theatre) entracte, l' (m) *oñtrakt*
introduce (v.) présenter *prayzoñtay*
iron fer à repasser, le *fer a ruhpasay*
is est *ay*
is not n'est pas *nay pa*
it is c'est *say*
it's okay; I am/you are okay ça va *sa va*

J

jack (car) cric, le *kreek*
jar pot, le *poh*
jewel bijou, le *beejoo*
jeweller's bijouterie, la *beejootree*
job travail, le *traviy*
journey voyage, le *vwiyaj*
juice jus, le *jew*
jump (v.) sauter *sohtay*
junction croisement, le *krwazmoñ*

K

keep (v.) garder *garday*
keep to the right serrez à droite *seray a drwat*
key clé, la *klay*
key in one's PIN (v.) taper son code secret *tapay sawñ kod suhkray*
key ring porte-clés, le *portuhklay*
kilogram kilo, le *keeloh*
kind gentil/gentille; aimable *joñtee/joñteey; aymabl*
kitchen cuisine, la *kweezeen*
knee genou, le *juhnoo*
knife couteau, le *kootoh*

L

lace dentelle, la *doñtel*
lady dame, la *dam*
lamp lampe, la *loñp*
laptop ordinateur portable, l' (m) *ordeenatuhr portabl*
large grand(e); gros/grosse *groñ/groñd; groh/grohs*
last dernier/dernière *dernyay/dernyer*
last (v.) durer *dewray*
late tard *tar*
later plus tard *plew tar*
lawyer avocat(e), l' (m/f) *avohka/avohkat*
layer couche, la *koosh*
lead (heavy metal) plomb, le *plawñ*
leaf feuille, la *fuhy*
leather cuir, le *kweer*
leather goods maroquinerie, la *marokeenree*
leave (go away) (v.) partir *parteer*
leave (behind) (v.) laisser *laysay*
left (opp. of right) gauche, la *gohsh*
left-luggage office consigne, la *kawñseeny*
leg jambe, la *joñb*

leisure loisirs, les (mpl) *lwazeer*
lens lentille, la *loñteey*
lentil lentille, la *loñteey*
less moins *mwañ*
lesson cours, le *koor*
let (allow) (v.) laisser *laysay*
letter lettre, la *letr*
licence permis, le *permee*
lifeguard surveillant(e) de baignade, le/la *sewrvayyoñ/sewrvayyoñt duh baynyad*
lifejacket gilet de sauvetage, le *jeelay duh sohvtaj*
lift ascenseur, l' (m) *asoñsuhr*
lift (v.) lever *luhvay*
light lumière, la *lewmyer*
light (colour) clair(e) *kler*
light (not heavy) léger/légère *layjay/layjer*
light bulb ampoule, l' (f) *oñpool*
lighthouse phare, le *far*
lights (on car) feux, les (mpl); phares, les (mpl) *fuh; far*
like comme *kom*
line ligne, la *leeny*
linen (sheets, etc.) linge, le *lañj*
liqueur liqueur, la *leekuhr*
liquid liquide, le *leekeed*
litre litre, le *leetr*
little (small amount) peu *puh*
little (small) petit(e) *puhtee/puhteet*
liver foie, le *fwa*
loaf pain, le *pañ*
lock serrure, la *serewr*
long long/longue *lawñ/lawñg*
(a) long time longtemps *lawñtoñ*
lose (v.) perdre *perdr*
lost perdu(e) *perdew*
lounge salon, le *salawñ*
low bas/basse *ba/bas*
lunch déjeuner, le *dayjuhnay*
lung poumon, le *poomawñ*
lying down allongé(e) *alawñjay*

M

make (v.) faire *fer*
man homme, l' (m) *hom*
map carte, la; plan, le *kart;ploñ*
market marché, le *marshay*
married marié(e) *maryay*
mask masque, le *mask*
match allumette, l' (f) *alewmet*
matt (finish) mat(e) *mat*
mattress matelas, le *matla*
meal repas, le *ruhpa*
measles rougeole, la *roojol*
meat viande, la *vyoñd*
medicine médicament, le *maydeekamoñ*
memory card carte mémoire, la *kart maymwar*

menu carte, la; menu, le (fixed price) *kart; muhnew*

meter compteur, le *kawñtuhr*

midday midi *meedee*

midnight minuit *meenwee*

milk lait, le *lay*

milkshake milkshake, le *meelkshek*

minibar minibar, le *meeneebar*

Miss Mademoiselle (f) *madmwazel*

mistake erreur, l' (f) *eruhr*

mobile phone (téléphone) portable, le *(taylayfon) portabl*

money argent, l' (m) *arjoñ*

month mois, le *mwa*

more plus *plews*

morning matin, le; matinée, la *matañ; mateenay*

mother mère, la *mer*

motor home camping-car, le *koñpeeng kar*

motorway autoroute, l' (f) *ohtohroot*

mouth bouche, la *boosh*

move (v.) bouger *boojay*

MP3-player lecteur mp3, le *lektuhr empaytrwa*

Mr/Sir Monsieur *muhsyuh*

Mrs/Madam Madame (f) *madam*

much/many beaucoup *bohkoo*

multiple sclerosis sclérose en plaques, la *sklayrohz oñ plak*

museum musée, le *mewzay*

music musique, la *mewzeek*

N

name nom, le *nawñ*

napkin serviette, la *servyet*

nappy couche, la *koosh*

natural (e.g. yoghurt) nature *natewr*

nausea nausée, la *nohzay*

near près (de) *pre (duh)*

nearest plus proche *plew prosh*

nec cou, le *koo*

necklace collier, le *kolyay*

nectarine nectarine, la *nektareen*

need (v.) avoir besoin de *avwar buhzwañ duh*

neighbourhood quartier, le *kartyay*

neither ... nor ni ... ni *nee ... nee*

never (ne ...) jamais *(nuh ...) jamay*

new nouveau/nouvelle *noovoh/noovel*

newspaper journal, le *joornal*

next prochain(e) *proshañ/proshen*

night nuit, la *nwee*

nightclub boîte (de nuit), la *bwat (duh nwee)*

no non *nawñ*

no longer, no more ne ... plus *nuh ... plew*

no through road impasse, l' (f) *añpas*

nobody ne ... personne *nuh ... person*

north nord, le *nor*

nose nez, le *nay*

not ne ... pas *nuh ... pa*

note (musical/written) note, la *noht*

nothing ne ... rien *nuh ... ryañ*

number numéro, le *newmayroh*

numbered numéroté(e) *newmayrotay*

nurse infirmier/infirmière, l' (m/f) *añfeermyay/añfeermyer*

O

oar rame, la *ram*

obtain (v.) obtenir *obtuhneer*

o'clock heure(s) *uhr*

occupied occupé(e) *okewpay*

of course bien sûr *byañ sewr*

office bureau, le *bewroh*

often souvent *soovoñ*

oil/vinegar cruet huilier, l' (m) *weelyay*

ointment pommade, la *pomad*

okay d'accord *dakor*

old vieux/vieille *vyuh/vyey*

on sur *sewr*

once une fois *ewn fwa*

one un(e) *uñ/ewn*

one-way street (rue à) sens unique *(rew a) soñs ewneek*

only seulement; ne ... que *suhlmoñ; nuh ... kuh*

open (v.) ouvrir *oovreer*

open/opened ouvert(e) *oover/oovert*

operation opération, l' (f) *opayrasyawñ*

opposite en face de *oñ fas duh*

or ou *oo*

orange orange, l' (f) *oroñj*

orchestra orchestre, l' (m) *orkestr*

order (v.) commander *komoñday*

organic food produits biologiques, les (mpl) *prodwee beeolojeek*

original language film version originale, la *versyawñ oreejeenal*

other autre *ohtr*

out of order en panne *oñ pan*

over there là-bas *laba*

owner patron le/patronne, la *patrawñ/patron*

P

pacemaker stimulateur cardiaque, le *steemewlatuhr kardyak*

packet paquet, le; plaquette, la (butter) *pakay; plaket*

painkiller analgésique, l' (m) *analjayzeek*

pain mal, le *mal*

paint/painting peinture, la *pañtewr*

pancake (sweet; savoury) crêpe, la; galette, la *krep/galet*

paper papier, le *papyay*
parade défilé, le *dayfeelay*
parasol parasol, le *parasol*
park parc, le *park*
park (v.) garer; se garer *garay; suh garay*
parking stationnement, le *stasyonmoñ*
partner compagnon, le/compagne, la
   kawñpanyawñ/kawñpany
pass (v.) passer *pasay*
passport passeport, le *paspor*
path chemin, le *shuhmañ*
pattern motif, le *mohteef*
pay (v.) payer *payyay*
pedal pédale, la *paydal*
pedestrian piéton, le/piétonne, la
   pyaytawñ/pyayton
people gens, les (mpl) *joñ*
per par *par*
perfume parfum, le *parfañ*
period (menstrual) règles, les (fpl) *regl*
person personne, la *person*
petrol essence, l' (f) *esoñs*
petrol station station-service, la *stasyawñ
   servees*
phone card télécarte, la *taylaykart*
pick up (v.) ramasser *ramasay*
piece morceau, le *morsoh*
pink rose *rohz*
pitch (on campsite) emplacement, l' (m)
   oñplasmoñ
place setting couvert, le *koover*
plain (e.g. omelette) nature *natewr*
plain (e.g. colour) uni(e) *ewnee*
plan (map) plan, le *ploñ*
plank planche, la *ploñsh*
plate assiette, l' (f) *asyet*
platform quai, le *kay*
play (v.) jouer *jooay*
please s'il vous plaît *seelvooplay*
pleased to meet you enchanté(e)
   oñshoñtay
pneumonia pneumonie, la *pnuhmonee*
police station commissariat, le *komeesarya*
pork porc, le *por*
pork butcher's charcuterie, la *sharkewtree*
portion portion, la *porsyawñ*
postcard carte postale, la *kart postal*
post office poste, la *post*
pot pot, le *poh*
power-assisted steering direction
   assistée, la *deereksyawñ aseestay*
pound livre, la *leevr*
pregnant enceinte *oñsañt*
prescription ordonnance, l' (f) *ordonoñs*
pressure pression, la *presyawñ*
pretty joli(e) *jolee*
price prix, le; tarif, le *pree; tareef*
product produit, le *prodwee*

programme programme, le *prohgram*
public public/publique *pewbleek*
pull (v.) tirer *teeray*
pull out (v.) arracher *arashay*
pullover pull, le *pewl*
puncture crevaison, la *kruhvayzawñ*
purse porte-monnaie, le *portuhmonay*
put (v.) mettre *metr*

Q
quarter quart, le *kar*
quickly vite *veet*
quiet tranquille *troñkeel*

R
race course, la *koors*
racket raquette, la *raket*
radiator radiateur, le *radyatuhr*
rambling randonnée pédestre, la *roñdonay
   paydestr*
ramp rampe (d'accès), la *roñp (daxe)*
rash rougeur, la *roojuhr*
rate taux, le *toh*
razor rasoir, le *razwar*
ready prêt(e) *pre/pret*
receipt reçu, le; ticket de caisse, le
   ruhsew; teekay duh kes
recommend (v.) conseiller; recommander
   kawñsayyay; ruhkomoñday
red rouge *rooj*
reflect (think) (v.) réfléchir *rayflaysheer*
regional régional(e) *rayjyonal*
registration (car) immatriculation, l' (f)
   eematreekewlasyawñ
remain (v.) rester *restay*
reminder rappel, le *rapel*
rent loyer, le *lwiyay*
rent (v.) louer *looay*
reservation réservation, la *rayzervasyawñ*
reserve (v.) réserver *rayzervay*
rest (relaxation) repos, le *ruhpoh*
rest (remainder) reste, le *rest*
restaurant restaurant, le *restohroñ*
return ticket aller-retour, l' (m) *allay
   ruhtoor*
rib côte, la *koht*
right (opp. of left) droite, la *drwat*
ring bague, la *bag*
ripe mûr(e) *mewr*
risk risque, le *reesk*
road route, la *root*
rock climbing varappe, la *varap*
rollerblades patins en ligne, les (mpl)
   patañ oñ leeny
room salle, la; chambre, la **(in hotel)**
   sal; shoñbr
room service service en chambre, le
   servees oñ shoñbr
roundabout rond-point, le *rawñpwañ*

rowing aviron, l' (m) *aveerawñ*
rubbish ordures, les (fpl) *ordewr*
rucksack sac à dos, le *sak a doh*
rule règlement, le *regluhmoñ*
run (v.) courir *kooreer*

S

safe deposit box coffre-fort, le *kofruhfor*
sail voile, la *vwal*
sailing dinghy dériveur, le *dayreevuhr*
sales soldes, les (m) *sohld*
sales executive cadre commercial, le *kadr komersyal*
same même *mem*
sand sable, le *sabl*
sandwich sandwich, le *soñdweetsh*
satisfied satisfait(e) *sateesfay/sateesfet*
scarf foulard, le *foolar*
school école, l' (f) *aykol*
scuba diving plongée sous-marine, la *plawñjay soo mareen*
sculpture sculpture, la *skewlptewr*
sea mer, la *mer*
seasickness mal de mer, le *mal duh mer*
season saison, la *sayzawñ*
seat (on bus, at theatre) place, la *plas*
see (v.) voir *vwar*
see you tomorrow à demain *a duhmañ*
self-catering flat/cottage appartement, l' (m); gîte meublé, le *apartuhmoñ; jeet muhblay*
self-service libre-service, le; self-service, le *leebr-servees; self-servees*
sell (v.) vendre *voñdr*
send (v.) envoyer *oñvwiyay*
senior citizen personne âgée, la *person ajay*
sense (v.) sentir *soñteer*
serious grave *grav*
service service, le *servees*
set price forfait, le *forfay*
shampoo shampooing, le *shoñpwañ*
sheet (for bed) drap, le *dra*
sheet (paper) feuille, la *fuhy*
shelf (section in shop) rayon, le *rayawñ*
shiny brillant(e) *breeyoñ/breeyoñt*
shirt chemise, la *shuhmeez*
shoe chaussure, la *shohsewr*
shoe size pointure, la *pwañtewr*
shop magasin, le *magazañ*
shopkeeper marchand(e), le/la *marshoñ/marshoñd*
shopping centre centre commercial, le *soñtr komersyal*
short court(e) *koor/koort*
shoulder épaule, l' (f) *aypohl*
show (v.) montrer *mawñtray*
shower douche, la *doosh*

shutter volet, le *volay*
shuttle navette, la *navet*
side dish accompagnement, l' (m) *akoñpanymoñ*
silk soie, la *swa*
silver argent, l' (m) *arjoñ*
since (time) depuis *duhpwee*
single (unmarried) célibataire *sayleebater*
single ticket aller simple, l' (m) *alay sañpl*
sinus infection sinusite, la *seenewzeet*
size taille, la *tiy*
skates patins, les (mpl) *patañ*
ski slope piste, la *peest*
skiing (cross-country/downhill) ski (de fond/de piste), le *skee (duh fawñ/duh peest)*
skirt jupe, la *jewp*
sledge luge, la *lewj*
sleeping bag sac de couchage, le *sak duh kooshaj*
sleeping car wagon-lit, le *vagawñ lee*
sleeve manche, la *moñsh*
slice tranche, la *troñsh*
slice (v.) trancher *troñshay*
slow lent(e) *loñ/loñt*
slow down (v.) ralentir *raloñteer*
slowly lentement *loñtuhmoñ*
small petit(e) *puhtee/puhteet*
smell (v.) sentir *soñteer*
smoke (v.) fumer *fewmay*
smoker fumeur, le/fumeuse, la *fewmuhr/fewmuhz*
snowboarding snowboard, le *snohbord*
so alors *alor*
soap savon, le *savawñ*
sock chaussette, la *shohset*
soft mou/molle *moo/mol*
some du (m)/de la (f)/des (mpl/fpl) *dew/duh la/day*
someone quelqu'un *kelkuñ*
son fils, le *fees*
sorry désolé(e); pardon *dayzohlay; pardawñ*
sort sorte, la *sort*
sort (v.) (household waste) trier (les déchets) *treeay*
south sud, le *sewd*
spark plug bougie, la *boojee*
sparkling (wine) mousseux *moosuh*
speak (v.) parler *parlay*
speciality spécialité, la *spaysyaleetay*
speed vitesse, la *veetes*
spend (time) (v.) passer *pasay*
spicy épicé(e) *aypeesay*
spine colonne vertébrale, la *kolon vertaybral*

spirits (drinks) spiritueux, les (mpl) *speereetewuh*
spoon cuillère, la *kweeyer*
sport sport, le *spor*
sprain entorse, l' (f) *oñtors*
square (in town) place, la *plas*
squeezed (e.g. lemon) pressé(e) *presay*
stadium stade, le *stad*
stairs escalier, l' (m) *eskalyay*
stalls (theatre) orchestre, l' (m) *orkestr*
stamp timbre, le *tañbr*
start up (car) (v.) démarrer *daymaray*
station gare, la *gar*
stationer's papeterie, la *papetree*
stay séjour, le *sayjoor*
stay (v.) rester *restay*
steal (v.) voler *volay*
steam vapeur, la *vapuhr*
steamed à la vapeur *a la vapuhr*
steering wheel volant, le *voloñ*
sticky adhésif/adhésive *adayzeef/adayzeev*
still encore; toujours *oñkor; toojoor*
sting piqûre, la *peekewr*
stomach estomac, l' (m) *estoma*
stop arrêt, l' (m) *aray*
stop (oneself/itself) s'arrêter *saretay*
storey étage, l' (m) *aytaj*
straight droit(e) *drwa/drwat*
straight on tout droit *too drwa*
straw paille, la *piy*
street rue, la *rew*
string ficelle, la *feesel*
strong fort(e); serré(e) (for coffee) *for/fort; seray*
student étudiant(e), l' (m/f) *aytewdyoñ/ aytewdyoñt*
stung piqué(e) *peekay*
subtitle sous-titre, le *soo teetr*
sugar sucre, le *sewkr*
sun soleil, le *soley*
sunburn coup de soleil, le *koo duh soley*
sunstroke insolation, l' (f) *añsolasyawñ*
suppository suppositoire, le *sewpozeetwar*
swallow (v.) avaler *avalay*
sweet bonbon, le *bawñbawñ*
swim (v.) nager *najay*
swimming pool piscine, la *peeseen*
swimsuit maillot (de bain), le *miyoh (duh bañ)*
syrup sirop, le *seeroh*

T

table tennis ping-pong, le *peeng pawñg*
tablecloth nappe, la *nap*
tablet cachet, le *kashay*
tablet comprimé, le *kawñpreemay*
take (v.) prendre *proñdr*
take away (v.) emporter *oñportay*

tall grand(e) *groñ/groñd*
tap (water) (eau du) robinet, le *(oh dew) robeenay*
tariff tarif, le *tareef*
taste (v.) goûter *gootay*
tasting (food/wine) dégustation, la *daygewstasyawñ*
taxes taxes, les (fpl) *tax*
taxi taxi, le *taxee*
tea thé, le *tay*
teacher professeur, le *profesuhr*
telephone téléphone, le *taylayfon*
temperature température, la; fièvre, la (fever) *toñpayratewr; fyayvr*
temporary provisoire *proveezwar*
thank you merci *mersee*
that ce (m)/cette (f); ça *suh/set; sa*
the le (m)/la (f)/les (mpl/fpl) *luh/la/lay*
theft vol, le *vol*
then puis; alors *pwee; alor*
there là *la*
there is/there are il y a *eelya*
there it is voilà *vwala*
these ces (mpl/fpl) *say*
thigh cuisse, la *kwees*
thing chose, la *shohz*
think about (v.) réfléchir *rayflaysheer*
third (portion) tiers, le *tyer*
this ce (m)/cette (f) *suh/set*
those ces (mpl/fpl) *say*
throat gorge, la *gorj*
ticket billet, le *beeyay*
ticket office guichet, le *geeshay*
tide marée, la *maray*
tie cravate, la *kravat*
tight serré(e) *seray*
tights collant, le *koloñ*
time (general) temps, le *toñ*
time (specific; of the clock) heure, l' (f) *uhr*
timetable horaire, l' (m) *orer*
tin boîte, la *bwat*
tinned food conserves, les (fpl) *kawñserv*
tobacco tabac, le *taba*
tobacconist bureau de tabac, le *bewroh duh taba*
today aujourd'hui *ohjoordwee*
toilets toilettes, les (fpl) *twalet*
toll péage, le *payaj*
tomorrow demain *duhmañ*
tongue langue, la *loñg*
too (much) trop *troh*
tooth dent, la *doñ*
tooth filling plombage, le *plawñbaj*
toothpaste dentifrice, le *doñteefrees*
top-up card (for mobile phone) carte recharge, la *kart ruhsharj*
tough dur(e) *dewr*
tour tour, le *toor*

tournament tournoi, le *toornwa*
tow rope câble de remorquage, le *kabl duh ruhmorkaj*
towel serviette, la *servyet*
tower tour, la *toor*
town ville, la *veel*
town centre centre-ville, le *soñtr veel*
toy jouet, le *jooay*
track piste, la *peest*
traffic lights feux, les *fuh*
traveller's cheque chèque de voyage, le; traveller, le *shek duh vvwiyaj; travluhr*
treatment sheet feuille de soins, la *fuhy duh swañ*
trip voyage, le *vvwiyaj*
trousers pantalon, le *poñtalawñ*
try (v.) essayer *esayyay*
tummy ventre, le *voñtr*
tuna thon, le *tawñ*
turn (v.) tourner *toornay*
twice deux fois *duh fwa*
type sorte, la *sort*
tyre pneu, le *pnuh*

U

ulcer ulcère, l' (m) *ewlser*
understand (v.) comprendre *kawñproñdr*
unfortunately malheureusement *maluhruhzmoñ*
united uni(e) *ewnee*
unlimited illimité(e) *eeleemeetay*
until jusqu'à/au/aux *jewska/jewskoh*

V

validate a ticket (v.) composter *kawñpostay*
vegan végétalien/végétalienne *vayjaytalyañ/vayjaytalyen*
vegetarian végétarien/végétarienne *vayjaytaryañ/vayjaytaryen*
veil voile, la *vvwal*
ventilation aération, l' (f) *aayrasyawñ*
vertigo vertige, le *verteej*
very très *tre*
vomit (v.) vomir *vomeer*

W

wafer gaufrette, la *gohfret*
waffle gaufre, la *gohfr*
wait (for) (v.) attendre *atoñdr*
walk (v.) marcher *marshay*
wall (around city) rempart, le *roñpar*
wallet portefeuille, le *portuhfuhy*
want (v.) vouloir; désirer *voolwar; dayzeeray*
washbasin lavabo, le *lavaboh*
washing lessive, la; linge, le *leseev; lañj*

washing powder lessive, la *lesseev*
watch montre, la *mawñtr*
watch out! attention! *atoñsyawñ*
water eau, l' (f) *oh*
waterskiing ski nautique, le *skee nohteek*
way (in directions) chemin, le *shuhmañ*
weak (drink) léger/légère *layjay/layjer*
weather temps, le *toñ*
week semaine, la *suhmen*
weight poids, le *pwa*
well bien *byañ*
west ouest, l' (m) *ooest*
what is it? qu'est-ce que c'est? *keskuh say*
what is there?/what's wrong? qu'est-ce qu'il y a? *keskeelya*
wheat blé, le *blay*
wheel roue, la *roo*
wheelchair fauteuil roulant, le *fohtuhy roolloñ*
when quand *koñ*
where où *oo*
which? quel/quelle? *kel*
which one? lequel?/laquelle? *luhkel/lakel*
white blanc/blanche *bloñ/bloñsh*
white coffee crème, le *krem*
who qui *kee*
whole entier/entière *oñtyay/oñtyer*
wholemeal (bread) complet *kawñple*
why? pourquoi? *poorkwa*
wife femme, la *fam*
windscreen pare-brise, le *par breez*
window fenêtre, la *fuhnetr*
windsurfing planche à voile, la *ploñsh a vval*
wine vin, le *vvañ*
with avec *avek*
without sans *soñ*
woman femme, la *fam*
wood bois, le *bwa*
wool laine, la *len*
work travail, le *traviy*
wrist poignet, le *pwanyay*
write (v.) écrire *aykreer*

X

x-ray radiographie, la *radyohgrafee*

Y

yellow jaune *john*
yes oui *wee*
yesterday hier *eeyer*
young jeune *juhn*
you're welcome de rien *duh ryañ*
youth jeunesse, la *juhnes*

A

à at/to
à demain see you tomorrow
à la vapeur steamed
à partir de from (with times and dates)
abcès, l' (m) abcess
accélérateur, l' (m) accelerator
accompagnement, l' (m) side dish
d'accord agreed; okay
acheter to buy
addition, l' (f) bill
adhésif/adhésive sticky
adresse, l' (f) address
adulte, l' (m/f) adult
aération, l' (f) ventilation
aéroport, l' (m) airport
agence (immobilière), l' (f) (estate)
  agency
aide to help
aimable helpful; kind
air, l' (m) air
ajouter to add
alcoolisé(e) alcoholic
alimentation générale, l' (f) grocer's shop
aller to go
aller-retour, l' (m) return ticket
aller simple, l' (m) single ticket
allergique allergic
allongé(e) lying down
allumette, l' (f) match; thinly cut chip
alors so; then
ambulance, l' (f) ambulance
américain(e) American
américain, l' (m) ham salad sandwich
ampoule, l' (f) blister; light bulb
analgésique, l' (m) painkiller
anglais(e) English
animal, l' (m) animal
antibiotique, l' (m) antibiotics
apéritif, l' (m) aperitif
appareil-photo (jetable/numérique), l'
  (m) (disposable/digital) camera
appartement, l' (m) apartment; flat
appartement meublé, l' (m) self-catering
  flat
appel, l' (m) call
appeler to call
appendicite, l' (f) appendicitis
appétit, l' (m) appetite
appliquer to apply
apporter to bring
après after
après-midi, l' (m/f) afternoon
argent, l' (m) money; silver
arracher to extract; to pull out
arrêt, l' (m) stop
art, l' (m) art

ascenseur, l' (m) lift
aspirine, l' (f) aspirin
assez enough; fairly
assiette, l' (f) plate
assurance, l' (f) insurance
asthme, l' (m) asthma
atelier, l' (m) craft workshop
attendre to wait (for)
attention! watch out!; be careful
attraction, l' (f) amusement
au (m) at the; to the
au secours! help!
auberge, l' (f) inn
aujourd'hui today
autoroute, l' (f) motorway
autre other
aux (mpl/fpl) at the; to the
avaler to swallow
avant before
avant-hier the day before yesterday
avec with
aveugle blind
avion, l' (m) aeroplane
avocat, l' (m) avocado
avocat(e), l' (m/f) lawyer
avoir to have
avoir besoin de to need
avoir mal to have a pain

B

bague, la ring
baguette, la long French loaf
baignoire, la bathtub
bain, le bath
balade, la stroll
balcon, le balcony/circle (theatre)
balle, la small ball; bullet
ballet, le ballet
ballon, le large ball; balloon
banc, le bench
banque, la bank
bar, le bar
bas/basse low
bateau, le boat
batterie, la battery (car); drums (music)
beau/belle beautiful
beaucoup much; many; a lot
beauté, la beauty
bidet, le bidet
bien well; good
bien sûr of course
bijou, le jewel
bijouterie, la jeweller's
billet, le ticket; banknote
biscuit, le biscuit
blanc/blanche white
blé, le wheat
bleu(e) blue

blonde, la lager (beer)
boire to drink
bois, le wood
boisson, la drink
boîte, la box; tin; can; nightclub
boîte de vitesses, la gear box
bon/bonne good
bonbon, le sweet
bonjour hello
bonsoir good evening
bouche, la mouth
boucherie, la butcher's shop
bouchon, le cork
boucle d'oreille, la earring
bouée, la buoy; rubber ring
bouger to move
bougie, la candle; spark plug
boulangerie, la bakery
bouteille, la bottle
bras, le arm
bricolage, le DIY
brillant(e) shiny; glossy
britannique British
bronchite, la bronchitis
brûlé(e) burnt
brûlure, la burn
brûlures d'estomac, les (fpl) heartburn
brun(e) brown
bureau, le office
bureau de tabac, le tobacconist
bus, le bus

C

ça that; it
ça va it's okay; I am/you are okay
cabillaud, le cod
câble de remorquage, le tow rope
cacahuètes, les (fpl) peanuts
cacao, le cocoa
cachet, le tablet
cadeau, le gift
caisse, la checkout, till
caméscope, le camcorder
campagne, la countryside
camper to camp
camping, le camping
camping-car, le motor home
canot, le dinghy
car, le coach; bus
caravane, la caravan
carnaval, le carnival
carrefour, le crossroads
carte, la map; card; menu
carte mémoire, la memory card
carte postale, la postcard
carte recharge, la top-up card (for mobile phone)
carton, le carton; cardboard

cassé(e) broken
caution, la deposit
ce (m) this; that
cédez (le passage) give way
ceinture, la belt
célibataire single (unmarried)
cendrier, le ashtray
centre commercial, le shopping centre
centre-ville, le town centre
ces (mpl/fpl) these/those
c'est it is/is it
cette (f) this/that
chaise, la chair
chaise haute, la high chair
chaise longue, la deckchair
chalet, le chalet; cottage
chambre, la bedroom; room (in hotel)
champ, le field
championnat, le championship
change, le exchange
changer to change
charcuterie, la pork butcher's; cold meat
château, le castle
chaud(e) hot
chaudière, la boiler
chauffage (central), le (central) heating
chaussette, la sock
chaussure, la shoe
chemin, le way; path
chemise, la shirt
chemisier, le blouse
chèque, le cheque
chèque de voyage, le traveller's cheque
cher/chère dear; expensive
cheval, le horse
cheville, la ankle
chose, la thing
cintre, le coathanger
cirque, le circus
clair(e) light (colour)
classique classical
clavicule, la collarbone
clé, la key
clientèle, la customers
climatisation, la air conditioning
club, le club
codes, les (mpl) dipped headlights
cœur, le heart
coffre-fort, le safe deposit box
coiffure, la hairdressing; hairstyle
coin, le corner
collant, le tights
colonne vertébrale, la spine
combien how much/many
commander to order
comme as; like
comment how

commissariat, le police station
commission, la commission
commotion cérébrale, la concussion
compagnon, le/compagne, la partner
complet/complète full; wholemeal (bread)
composter to validate a ticket
comprendre to understand
comprimé, le tablet
compris(e) included; understood
compteur, le meter
concert, le concert
conduire to drive
connexion internet, la internet connection
conseiller to advise; to recommend
conserves, les (fpl) tinned food
consigne, la left-luggage office
constipé(e) constipated
contagieux/contagieuse contagious
continuer to continue; to carry on
contre against
corbeille, la basket
correspondance, la connection
côte, la rib; coast
coton, le cotton
cou, le neck
couche, la nappy; layer
couleur, la colour
coup de soleil, le sunburn
coupe, la goblet; dish; cup (sport)
coupé(e) cut
courant, le current
courir to run
couronne, la crown
courroie de ventilateur, la fan belt
cours, le course; lesson; flow
course, la race; errand
court(e) short
couteau, le knife
couvert, le place setting
couverture, la blanket
cravate, la tie
crédit, le credit
crème, la cream
crème, le white coffee
crêpe, la (sweet) pancake
crevaison, la puncture
cric, le jack (car)
crise de foie, la overindulgence
croisement, le junction
cuillère, la spoon
cuir, le leather
cuisine, la kitchen
cuisinière, la cooker
cuisse, la thigh
cybercafé, le internet café
cycliste, le/la cyclist

D

d'accord agreed; okay
dame, la lady
dans in
date, la date (day)
de rien you're welcome
dedans inside; in it; in them
défense de forbidden
défilé, le parade
dégustation, la food/wine tasting
déjeuner, le lunch
délicieux/délicieuse delicious
demain tomorrow
démarrer to start up (car)
demi(e), le/la half
demi, le glass of beer (= half-pint)
demi-heure, la half an hour
demi-pension, la half board
dent, la tooth
dentelle, la lace
dentifrice, le toothpaste
dentiste, le/la dentist
dépannage, le breakdown service
depuis since; for
déranger to disturb
dériveur, le sailing dinghy
dernier/dernière last
derrière behind
des (mpl/fpl) some; any; of/from the
descendre to go/take down; to get off
désirer to want
désolé(e) sorry
dessert, le dessert
devant in front of
développer to develop
diabétique diabetic
diarrhée, la diarrhoea
direction (assistée), la direction; (power-
   assisted) steering
distractions, les (fpl) entertainment
distributeur automatique de billets, le
   cashpoint
dos, le back
double, le copy; double
douche, la shower
douzaine, la dozen
drap, le sheet
droit(e) straight
droite, la right (opposite of left)
du (m) some; any; of/from the
dur(e) hard; tough
durer to last

E

eau, l' (f) water
eau de Javel, l' (f) bleach
eau-de-vie, l' (f) brandy
échappement, l' (m) exhaust (car)

école, l' (f) school
écrire to write
effort, l' (m) effort
église, l' (f) church
électricité, l' (f) electricity
embrayage, l' (m) clutch
emplacement, l' (m) pitch (on campsite)
emporter to take away
en in; of it/them
en face (de) opposite
en panne out of order; broken down
en sus extra
enceinte pregnant
enchanté(e) pleased to meet you
encore again; still
enfant, l' (m/f) child
entier/entière whole
entorse, l' (f) sprain
entracte, l' (m) interval (theatre)
entrer to enter
environ about; approximately
envoyer to send
épaule, l' (f) shoulder
épicé(e) spicy
épicerie, l' (f) grocer's shop
épilepsie, l' (f) epilepsy
épileptique epileptic
équitation, l' (f) horse riding
erreur, l' (f) mistake
escalier, l' (m) stairs
escalier roulant, l' (m) escalator
espèces (fpl) cash
essayer to try
essence, l' (f) petrol
est, l' (m) east
est is
estomac, l' (m) stomach
et and
étage, l' (m) storey; level
étudiant(e), l' (m/f) student
excellent(e) excellent
excuser to excuse
exposition, l' (f) exhibition

F

faire to do; to make
faire le plein to fill up (petrol)
farine, la flour
fauteuil roulant, le wheelchair
femme, la woman; wife
fenêtre, la window
fer à repasser, le iron
ferme, la farm
fermer to close
fesse, la buttock
fête, la festivity; fair
fête foraine, la funfair
feu, le fire; traffic light

feu d'artifice, le fireworks
feuille, la leaf; sheet (paper)
feuille de soins, la treatment sheet
feux, les (mpl) (traffic) lights; fires
fiche, la form
fièvre, la temperature (fever)
fille, la girl; daughter
fils, le son
filtre, le filter
finir to finish
flacon, le small bottle
flotteur, le armband; float
foie, le liver
foire, la fair
une/deux fois once/twice
foncé(e) dark (colour)
foot(ball), le football
forcer to force; to break into
forfait, le set price; all-in deal
fort(e) strong
foulard, le scarf
fracture, la fracture; break
frais/fraîche fresh; cool
français(e) French
frappé(e) iced (coffee)
frein, le brake
froid(e) cold (temperature)
fromage, le cheese
fruit, le fruit
fumer to smoke
fumeur, le/fumeuse, la smoker

G

galerie, la gallery
galette, la savoury pancake
garage, le garage
garçon, le boy
garder to keep
gare, la station
garer; se garer to park
garni(e) garnished
gâteau, le cake
gauche, la left (opposite of right)
gaufre, la waffle
gaufrette, la wafer
gaz, le gas
gazeux/gazeuse fizzy
général(e) general
généraliste, le GP; doctor
genou, le knee
gens, les (mpl) people
gentil/gentille kind
gilet de sauvetage, le life jacket
gîte meublé, le self-catering cottage
glace, la ice; ice cream
glacier, le ice cream parlour; glacier
glaçon, le ice cube
golf, le golf

gorge, la throat
goûter to taste
grand(e) tall; large
gratuit(e) free of charge
grave serious
gravillons, les (mpl) loose chippings
grippe, la 'flu; influenza
gris(e) grey
gros/grosse big; large
gueule de bois, la hangover
guichet, le ticket office; counter
guide, le guide (person); guidebook

H

halles, les (f) covered market
haut(e) high
heure, l' (f) hour; time
hier yesterday
homme, l' (m) man
hôpital, l' (m) hospital
horaire, l' (m) timetable
hôte/hôtesse, l' (m/f) host/hostess
hôtel, l' (m) hotel
huilier, l' (m) oil/vinegar cruet

I

ici here
il faut it is necessary; we need; you must
il y a there is/there are
illimité(e) unlimited
immatriculation, l' (f) (car) registration
impasse, l' (f) dead end,
inclus(e) included
indigestion, l' (f) indigestion
infection, l' (f) infection
infirmier/infirmière, l' (m/f) nurse
informatique, l' (f) computing
infusion, l' (f) herbal tea
insecte, l' (m) insect
insolation, l' (f) sunstroke
interdit(e) forbidden
intéressant(e) interesting

J

j'ai I have
jamais never
jambe, la leg
jambon, le ham
jardin, le garden
jaune yellow
je I
jeune young
jeunesse, la youth
joli(e) pretty
jouer to play
jouet, le toy
jour, le day
journal, le newspaper
jupe, la skirt

jus, le juice
jusqu'à/au/aux up to; until; as far as

K

kilo, le kilogram

L

la the; it; her
là there
là-bas over there
laine, la wool
laisser to leave (behind); to let (allow)
lait, le milk
lampe, la lamp
langue, la tongue
laquelle? (f) which one?
lavabo, le wash basin
le the; it; him
lecteur mp3, le MP3-player
léger/légère light (not heavy); weak (drink)
lent(e) slow
lentement slowly
lentille, la lentil; (contact) lens
lequel? (m) which one?
les (mpl/fpl) the; them
lessive, la washing; washing powder
lettre, la letter
lever to lift
librairie, la bookshop
libre free
libre-service, le self-service
ligne, la line
linge, le linen (sheets); washing
liqueur, la liqueur
liquide, le liquid
lit, le bed
litre, le litre
livre, la pound
livre, le book
location, la hire, hiring
loge, la box (theatre)
loin far
loisirs, les (mpl) leisure
long/longue long
longtemps a long time
louer to hire; to rent; to let
lourd(e) heavy
loyer, le rent
luge, la sledge, toboggan
lumière, la light
lunettes, les (fpl) glasses

M

Madame (f) Mrs; Madam
Mademoiselle (f) Miss
magasin, le shop
maillot (de bain), le swimsuit
main, la hand

mais but
maison, la house; family firm
maison homemade
mal badly
mal, le pain; ache; sickness
mal de mer, le seasickness
malheureusement unfortunately
manche, la sleeve
Manche, la English Channel
manger to eat
manteau, le coat
marchand(e), le/la shopkeeper
marché, le market
marcher to walk; to function
marée, la tide
mari, le husband
marié(e) married
maroquinerie, la leather goods
marque, la brand
marron, le brown; chestnut
masque, le mask
mat(e) matt (finish)
matelas, le mattress
matin, le morning
matinee, la afternoon performance; morning
mauvais(e) bad
médecin, le doctor
médicament, le medicine
même same; even
ménager/ménagère household
menu, le (fixed-price) menu
mer, la sea
merci thank you
mère, la mother
mettre to put
midi midday
millefeuilles, le vanilla cream slice
minibar, le minibar
minuit midnight
moins less; to (when telling the time)
mois, le month
moitié, la half
monnaie, la (small) change
Monsieur Mr; Sir
montre, la watch
montrer to show
morceau, le piece
motif, le pattern
mou/molle soft
mouchoir, le handkerchief
mousseux sparkling (wine)
mûr(e) ripe
musée, le museum
musique, la music

N

nager to swim
nappe, la tablecloth
nature plain; natural
nausée, la nausea
navette, la shuttle
ne ... jamais never
ne ... pas not
ne ... personne nobody
ne ... plus no more; no longer
ne ... que only
ne ... rien nothing
nectarine, la nectarine
n'est pas is not
neuf/neuve brand new
nez, le nose
ni ... ni neither ... nor
Noël Christmas
noir(e) black
nom, le name
non no
nord, le north
note, la bill; musical note
nouveau/nouvelle new
nuit, la night
numéro, le number
numéroté(e) numbered

O

obtenir to obtain
occupé(e) busy/occupied
œil, l' (m) eye
œufs, les (mpl) eggs
on we; you; someone; people
opération, l' (f) operation
orchestre, l' (m) orchestra; stalls (theatre)
ordinateur portable, l' (m) laptop
ordonnance, l' (f) prescription
ordures, les (fpl) rubbish
oreille, l' (f) ear
os, l' (m) bone
otite, l' (f) ear infection
ou or
où where
oublier to forget
ouest, l' (m) west
oui yes
ouvert(e) opened; open
ouvrir to open

P

paille, la straw
pain, le bread; loaf
palme, la flipper
panne, la breakdown
pansement, le dressing (medical)
pantalon, le trousers

papeterie, la stationer's
papier, le paper
paquet, le packet
paquet-cadeau, le gift-wrapped parcel
par by; per
parc, le park
pardon sorry
pare-brise, le windscreen
pare-chocs, le bumper
parfum, le perfume; flavour
parler to speak
partir to go away; to leave
passeport, le passport
passer to pass; to spend (time)
patinoire, la ice rink
patins (en ligne), les (mpl) skates
    (rollerblades)
pâtisserie, la cake shop; cakes
patron, le/patronne, la owner; boss
payer to pay
pays, le country; local region
péage, le toll
pêche, la peach; fishing
pédale, la pedal
peinture, la painting; paint
pellicule, la film (camera)
pension, la guest house; board
pension complète, la full board
perdre to lose
perdu(e) lost
permis, le licence
personne, la person
personne âgée, la senior citizen
pétanque, la petanque (bowls game)
petit(e) small; little
peu little (small amount)
phare, le headlight; lighthouse
pharmacie, la chemist's shop
pied, le foot
piéton, le/piétonne, la pedestrian
pile, la battery
ping-pong, le table tennis
piqué(e) stung
piqûre, la sting; injection
piscine, la swimming pool
piste, la track; ski slope
place, la seat; town square
plage, la beach
plan, le plan; map
planche, la board; plank
planche à voile, la windsurfing
plaquette, la packet (butter)/bar
    (chocolate)
plat, le dish
plein(e) full
plomb, le lead (heavy metal)
plombage, le tooth filling
plongée, la diving

plongée sous-marine, la scuba diving
plus more
plus tard later
pneu, le tyre
pneumatique inflatable
poids, le weight
poids lourd, le heavy goods vehicle
poignet, le wrist
pointure, la shoe size
poisson, le fish
poitrine, la chest; bust
pommade, la ointment
pont, le bridge
port, le harbour
porte, la door
porte-clés, le key ring
porte-monnaie, le purse
portefeuille, le wallet
portière, la (train/car) door
portion, la portion
poste, la post office
pot, le jar; pot
potable drinking (water)
poubelle, la (dust)bin
poumon, le lung
pour for; in order to
pourquoi why
pouvoir to be able
prélèvement, le sample
prendre to take
près near
présenter to introduce
préservatif, le condom
pressé(e) in a hurry; squeezed
pression, la draught beer; pressure
prêt(e) ready
prix, le price
prochain(e) next
proche near
produit, le product
produits biologiques/diététiques, les
    (mpl) organic/health food
produits laitiers, les (mpl) dairy products
professeur, le teacher
profond(e) deep
profondeur, la depth
programme, le programme
provisoire temporary
public/publique public
puis then
pull, le pullover

Q
quai, le platform
quand when
quart, le quarter
quartier, le neighbourhood
que that; which; what

quel/quelle? which?
quelqu'un someone; somebody
quetsche, la sweet purple plum
qui who; which
quincaillerie, la hardware (store)
qu'est-ce que c'est? what is it?
qu'est-ce qu'il y a? what is there?;
  what's wrong?

R

radiateur, le radiator
radiographie, la X-ray
ralentir to slow down
ramasser to pick up
rame, la oar
rampe (d'accès), la (access) ramp
randonnée pédestre, la hiking;
  rambling
rappel, le reminder
raquette, la racket
rasoir, le razor
rayon, le shelf; department (in shop)
recommander to recommend
reçu, le receipt
redevance, la fee
réfléchir to reflect; to think about
règlement, le rule
règles, les (fpl) (menstrual) period
rempart, le city wall
remplir to fill
rendez-vous, le appointment
repas, le meal
repos, le rest
réservation, la reservation
réserver to reserve
restaurant, le restaurant
reste, le rest
rester to remain; to stay
revenir to come back
rez-de-chaussée, le ground floor
rhume, le cold (medical complaint)
rideau, le curtain
rien nothing
risque, le risk
robe, la dress
robinet, le (water) tap
rond-point, le roundabout
rose pink
roue, la wheel
rouge red
rougeur, la rash
route, la road
rue, la street

S

sable, le sand
sac, le bag
sac à dos, le rucksack
sac de couchage, le sleeping bag
saison, la season
salle, la room
salle à manger, la dining room
salle de bains, la bathroom
salon, le lounge; living room
sandwich, le sandwich
sang blood
sans without
sans gluten gluten-free
s'appeler to be called
s'arrêter to stop (oneself)
satisfait(e) satisfied
saut à l'élastique, le bungee jumping
sauter to jump
savon, le soap
sclérose en plaques, la multiple sclerosis
sculpture, la sculpture
secours, le help
séjour, le stay
self-service, le self-service
semaine, la week
sens unique one-way (street)
sentir to smell; to feel; to sense
séropositif/séropositive HIV-positive
serré(e) tight; strong (coffee)
serrez à droite keep to the right
serrure, la lock
service, le service
service en chambre, le room service
serviette, la napkin; towel; briefcase
se trouver to be situated
seulement only
shampooing, le shampoo
s'il vous plaît please
sinusite, la sinus infection
sirop, le syrup
ski, le skiing
ski (de fond/de piste), le
  (cross-country/downhill) skiing
ski nautique, le water skiing
snowboard, le snowboarding
soie, la silk
soir, le evening
soldes, les (m) sales
soleil, le sun
somnolence, la drowsiness
sorte, la type; sort
sortie, la exit
sortir to go out
sourd(e) deaf
sous-sol, le basement
sous-titre, le subtitle
souvent often
spécialité, la speciality
spiritueux, les (mpl) spirits (drinks)
sport, le sport
stade, le stadium
station-service, la petrol station

stationnement, le parking
stimulateur cardiaque, le pacemaker
stores, les (mpl) blinds
sucette, la lollipop
sucre, le sugar
sud, le south
(en) supplément extra
suppositoire, le suppository
sur on
surgelés, les (mpl) frozen food
surveillant(e) de baignade, le/la lifeguard

T

tabac, le tobacco
table d'hôte, la evening meal provided
taille, la size
taper son code secret to key in one's PIN
tard late
tarif, le tariff; price
tasse, la cup
taux, le rate
taxes, les (fpl) taxes
taxi, le taxi
télécarte, la phone card
téléphone, le telephone
téléphone portable, le mobile phone
température, la temperature; fever
temps, le time; weather
tension, la blood pressure
terrain, le ground; course (golf)
terrain de camping, le campsite
tête, la head
thé, le tea
thon, le tuna
ticket de caisse, le receipt
tiers, le third (i.e. portion)
timbre, le stamp
tire-bouchon, le corkscrew
tirer to pull
tisane, la herb/fruit tea
toilettes, les (fpl) toilets
tour, la tower
tour, le tour
tourner to turn
tournoi, le tournament
tous (mpl)/toutes (fpl) all (pl)
tout(e) all
tout everything
tout de suite at once
tout droit straight on
toux, la cough
traiteur, le delicatessen
tranche, la slice
trancher to slice
tranquille quiet
travail, le job; work
traveller, le traveller's cheque
traversée, la crossing

traverser to cross
très very
trier (les déchets) to sort (household waste)
trop too (much)
trouver to find

U

ulcère, l' (m) ulcer
un(e) a; one
uni(e) plain (colour); united
usine, l' (f) factory

V

vacances, les (fpl) holidays
vapeur, la steam
varappe, la rock climbing
végétalien/végétalienne vegan
végétarien/végétarienne vegetarian
vélo, le bicycle
vendre to sell
venir to come
ventre, le tummy
verre, le glass
version française/originale, la dubbed/original language foreign film
vert(e) green
vertige, le dizziness; vertigo
vestiaire, le cloakroom; changing room
vêtements, les (mpl) clothes
viande, la meat
vieux/vieille old
ville, la town
vin, le wine
vite quickly
vitesse, la speed; gear (car)
voilà there; here it is
voile, la sail; veil
voir to see
voiture, la car
vol, le flight; theft
volant, le steering wheel
voler to steal; to fly
volet, le shutter
vomir to vomit; to be sick
voyage, le journey; trip

W

wagon-lit, le sleeping car

Y

yeux, les (mpl) eyes